GREAT TRAIN
DISASTERS

GREAT TRAIN DISASTERS

KEITH EASTLAKE

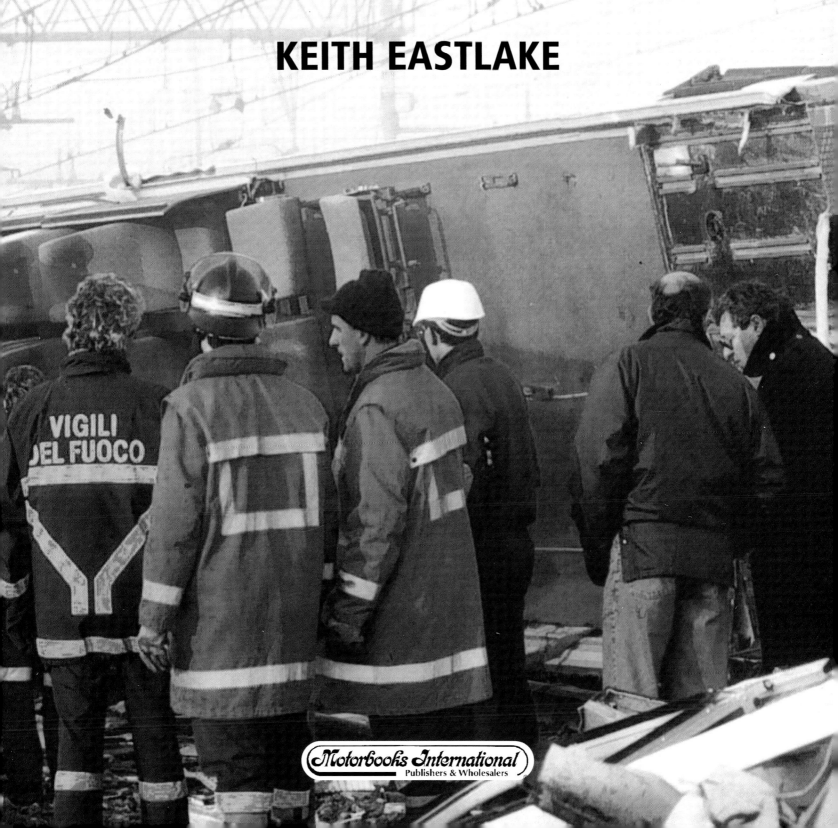

Motorbooks International
Publishers & Wholesalers

Library of Congress Cataloging-in-Publication Data Available.

ISBN 0-7603-0453-X

Printed and bound in Singapore

Photographic credits:
AFP Photo, pages: 25, 33, 45, 55(both), 56, 69, back cover
Arthur Trevena, page: 66(both)
Associated Press, pages: 28, 59
Boomsma Collection, page: 86
Corbis-Bettmann/UPI, pages: 20, 21(both), 41, 42(both), 43, 44(bottom), 46, 47(both), 63, 64(both), 65
HC Casserley, page: 66(both)
Hulton Getty Picture Collection Ltd, pages: 5, 6, 7(top) 12, 13(both), 15, 16, 22, 23(both), 26, 35, 36(both), 40(both), 48, 49, 50(both), 67, 70, 71(both), 72, 88, 90(both), 91
Hulton Getty Picture Collection Ltd/Reuter, pages: 11
Keystone, pages: 51, 83
Mary Evans Picture Library, pages: 34, 62, 84
MSI, pages: 57, 58(both)
Photo Source/Associated Press, pages: 1, 7(bottom)
Polfoto, page: 68
Popperfoto, pages: 19, 24, 27, 31, 38, 75, 76(both), 89
Popperfoto/Reuter, pages: 8, 29(both), 30, 52, 53, 54(both), 78(both), 81(top), 92, 93, 95(top)
Press Association, pages: 17, 18(both)
QA Photos Ltd, page: 77
Rex Features, pages: 2-3, 61, 73, 74(both), 79, 80, 81(bottom), 85, 94, 95(bottom)
Rex Features/Nils Jorgensen, page: front cover
Rex Features/Massimo Sestini, page: 9(bottom)
Rex Features/The Sun, page: 9(top)
Topham/Picturepoint, page: 39
Ullstein/Bilderdienst, pages: 37, 44(top), 87

Page 1: *French emergency staff remove passengers' belongings from the wreckage of the two trains involved in the crash at Argenton-sur-Creuse, France, on August 31, 1985.*

Pages 2-3: *Crash investigators and rail employees search through the remains of the Milan-Rome express following its derailment, January 1997.*

Below right: *The aftermath of the multiple collision at Harrow and Wealdstone station, London, October 1952.*

CONTENTS

INTRODUCTION

This book has been written as a general introduction to the history of tragedy on the world's railways in the twentieth century. The criteria on which accidents have been included have nothing to do with the numbers of dead and injured that an incident has produced, rather they are included because they highlight how a wide variety of defects, both mechanical and human, can lead to a disaster.

Rail transport remains one of the safest means of travelling between two places and our economies would not function without the vast volumes of freight and passengers carried by the networks, but it is not infallible. The history of the world's railways is littered with accidents that have shocked the public and occasionally highlighted the complacency of those who are responsible for the safe running of the networks. If any good can be said to come out of a tragedy, it is that complacency should not be a feature of those tasked with the transport of human beings. Safety consciousness and watchfulness have always been of paramount importance.

The book consists of four chapters and, while there is a measure of overlap particularly when a number of causes can be ascribed to a disaster, each looks at a specific type of tragedy. Collision between two or more trains is a not uncommon cause of an incident. Rail networks are run by humans, often highly skilled with years of training and work experience behind them, yet

Right: An injured passenger is removed from the wreckage of a Dutch train involved in a collision at Schiedam, May 1976.

Right: An injured passenger is removed from the wreckage of a Dutch train involved in a collision at Schiedam, May 1976.

Below: French rescue workers and crash investigators mill around the two trains involved in the accident at Argenton-sur-Creuse, August 1985.

they are prone to error, often brought about by stress, medical conditions, or wilful neglect of their duties. The technology that runs a system can range from the extremely simple to the bewilderingly complex, and it is certainly not foolproof. Anything, from a broken rail to faulty wiring in the most advanced form of signalling, can produce a failure in the system. Finally, rail networks are not immune to the vagaries of the natural environment or outside forces. Fog, flood, and fire have all played their part in initiating a rail accident. In nearly a century, there have been many hundreds of rail accidents, some large and headline grabbing, others insignificant. What they all reveal, however, is that accidents have many causes.

In many cases, the same factors behind an accident are evident whether the incident occurred at the beginning or end of the present century. In other cases, changes in technology have meant that the dangers inherent in an old system no longer apply because that system is no longer in operation.

However, every new technology brings its own potential problems. Where potential danger once lurked, today no threat is posed at all, but each new wave of technology brings its own problems. Only time and experience reveal if the replacement technology is equal to the demands placed upon it. Although new technology undergoes stringent safety checks before being introduced, it is often only in the light of its operational performance that any serious shortcomings can be identified and rectified.

Aspects common to all of the accidents discussed in this book are the response of the emergency services to an incident, and the enquiries that follow. Clearly, the speed of response of police, ambulance, and fire services has improved beyond measure since the beginning of the century, as has their ability to deliver high-quality medical aid to the injured. These highly skilled men and women work in some of the most appalling conditions, in darkness, in cramped tunnels or in thick acrid smoke, for example, and witness many horrifying scenes. Mistakes are sometimes made, but these are often brought about by the peculiarities of a particular accident and procedures are invariably reviewed in the light of experience.

Those tasked with uncovering the cause of an accident have become equally highly trained and are now aided by sophisticated technology. However, it remains crucial that they are able to distance themselves from the emotional impact of a disaster and analyse the evidence they gather with detachment. They have to ignore any public clamour for a witch-hunt and resist calls from interested parties or politicians to produce the 'correct' judgment. Rarely are they the judge and jury in a case, rather their job is to search out the cause of an incident and suggest ways in which a similar accident can be avoided in the future.

The depth and breadth of their findings and recommendations for improvements in safety regulations should also be viewed in the light of time and money. Modern railway safety devices, while vital, are costly

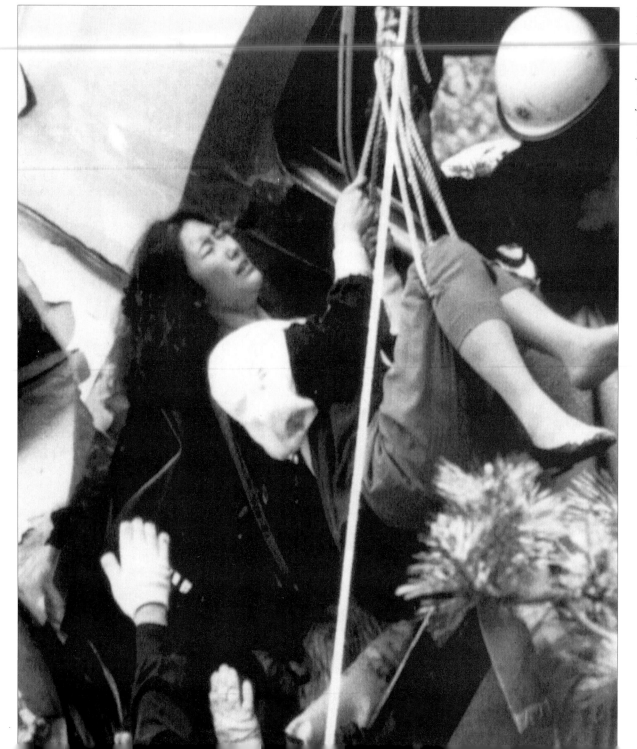

Left: A female passenger, clearly in considerable agony, is removed from the twisted wreck of a coach following the accident at Shigaraki, Japan, on May 14, 1991.

Left: *A burnt-out truck pictured after the fire in the Channel Tunnel, on November 21, 1996.*

and time-consuming to install, and no rail company has a bottomless wallet. Clear thinking has to be brought to bear on questions such as how much safety can be afforded. No one would seriously suggest neglecting safety in pursuit of profit but a balance has to be struck between the two. In a few instances, it is arguable that the balance has swung too far in favour of money rather than passengers, but such examples are rare.

However, general safety can be maintained by establishing and periodically reviewing procedures, and a strict policy of regular maintenance of track, signalling, and rolling stock will help reduce the likelihood of a serious incident. No system is 100 percent safe, but vigilance should ensure that the threat of disaster is sufficiently low as to maintain rail travel as one of the safest means of transport.

Right: *Italian fire officers and other members of the emergency services survey the wreck of the Milan-Rome express at Piacenza shortly after the crash of January 12, 1997.*

COLLISION

Violent collisions, whether head-on, rear-end, or side-impact, are the cause of some of the most frequent and devastating incidents on the world's railroad networks. The chance of severe casualties is great, not only because of the likely severity of the initial impact but also because of the possibility of other trains becoming involved, as was the case at Harrow and Wealdstone station in England on October 8, 1952, and the likelihood of further loss of life because of fire or violent explosion after the initial crash.

Collisions have many causes, from the plain stupidity of a passenger, as was the case with an off-duty soldier who pulled a communication cord to bring a Glasgow-Euston express to an unscheduled halt with catastrophic consequences, to the inexperience or misconduct of railroad employees. Signals can be misread or misinterpreted, or staff may not have received the training required to operate a new piece of railway technology.

In many cases, trains have been operating on a section of track under repair or improvement and have failed to take into account the potential dangers of following standard rules of conduct under changed circumstances. Some individuals may simply have ignored warnings or forgotten to follow established safety procedures when a train has been brought to an unscheduled stop. Drivers, guards, and signalmen have all proved fallible in these areas, often with serious consequences for their passengers and other staff members.

Right: The aftermath of a collision between Amtrak's 'Silver Meteor' and a large gas turbine which took place near Kissimmee, Florida, on November 26, 1993. Initial reports indicated more than 50 casualties in the smash.

SALISBURY, ENGLAND

JULY 1, 1906

This collision on the London and South Western Railway occurred shortly before 0200 hours one mid-summer morning, when the express boat-train travelling from the port of Plymouth in southwest England to Waterloo station in London failed to reduce speed while negotiating the sharply curving track at Salisbury station in Wiltshire. The boat train, which had been introduced just two years earlier to speed travellers to the capital, was carrying people who had crossed the Atlantic on a vessel owned by the America Line. At the time, it was the only train on the intercity line that did not stop at Salisbury station.

The boat train's locomotive and its passenger coaches left the track and crashed into a milk train passing through the station in the opposite direction. Railroad regulations of the time were meant to ensure that the Plymouth-Waterloo express passed through Salisbury at no more than 30mph (48km/h). Indeed, other regulations indicated that the train was supposed to negotiate the length of track between the station's two signal boxes at no more than 25mph (40km/h).

On this early July day, however, its speed was much higher, closer to the average for the complete high-speed journey from Plymouth to London. The violent impact resulted in 24 of the boat train's 43 passengers being killed, with many others suffering serious injuries. All the fatalities in the boat train where located in its three central cars and only five of its carriages remained undamaged following the smash.

Subsequent investigations revealed that the boat train's driver had attempted to negotiate the curving section of track at Salisbury station at a speed of over 60mph (96km/h). This was more than twice the official speed and was sufficient to topple the locomotive and bring it into contact with the milk train with such disastrous consequences. The board of investigation discov-

Below: Rail staff begin to clear the wreckage of the boat train from Salisbury station.

Right: Two steam-powered cranes start to clear some of the overturned debris from the main line through Salisbury.

ered that railroad companies at the time did not publish speed restrictions, such as the one supposedly in force at Salisbury, in the timetables available to their staff as a matter of course, and suggested that they should be introduced with some urgency, along with fitting speedometers in locomotives. The use of speedometers in trains did not become universal for almost another 50 years, however.

Passengers injured in the crash and the relatives of those killed received compensation of more than £23,000 some 12 months later, after the board of inves-

tigation had delivered its findings. However, one of the largest settlements, £7000, was agreed only in 1909 and went to a female traveller on the boat train.

The damage to the two trains themselves, however, was perhaps not as severe as might have been expected. Several of the worst effected passenger carriages on the express were scrapped following the investigation, but the locomotives themselves, some of the least damaged rolling stock, and track and other parts of Salisbury station were all repaired at a cost of a little over £5000.

Right: Railway staff attach heavy lifting chains to the engine of the boat train prior to it being removed from the scene of the accident.

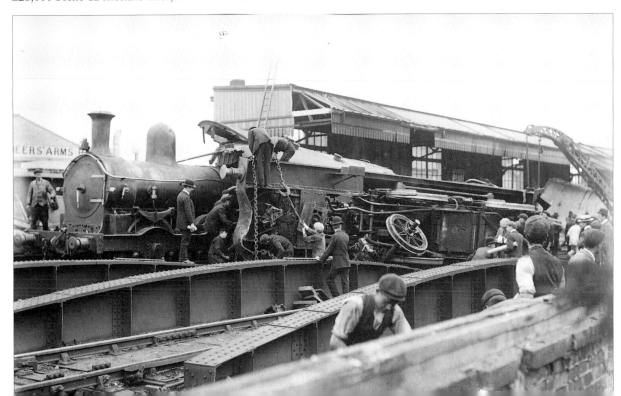

COLCHESTER, ENGLAND
JULY 12, 1913

This fatal collision in the East Anglian town could have been much worse except for the quick reactions of the driver of the Harwich train, one of two involved in this rear-end collision. Nevertheless, a large amount of rolling stock was smashed and several rail employees were killed when an express heading for Cromer on the north Norfolk coast hit the Harwich train at speed.

Below: The remains of the trains involved in the fatal collision at Colchester.

The Harwich goods train reached Colchester at 1411 hours, uncoupled, took on water, and was put at the disposal of the station for further duties. Because of the presence of a second train, the Harwich locomotive had to wait on the main line before being switched.

Unfortunately, due to a signalman's error, the Cromer express was allowed to continue on the same line as the stationary Harwich train, rather that waiting until the line ahead was cleared.

The Harwich train's driver sensed that something was wrong and sent his fireman to the signal box. At that moment, he spotted the Cromer express approaching at 40mph (64km/h) and attempted to get his locomotive under way. However, his train was struck and pushed nearly 300 yards (277m) along the track and then fell on its side. The express locomotive was badly damaged, with only its boiler being salvaged, and 14 people were injured, including the quick-thinking driver of the Harwich train.

SHRIVENHAM, ENGLAND

JANUARY 15, 1936

This collision on the Great Western Railway involved a coal train travelling from Aberdare to Old Oak Common and a nine-carriage sleeper making its way from Penzance in Cornwall to London's Paddington station. A collision between the two left two people dead and the chief investigator, Lieutenant-Colonel Mount, concluded that errors committed by two signalmen were the cause of the smash.

The incident began when the coal train pulling 53 full wagons broke in two a little time after passing through Swindon station. It had been a bitterly cold night, with frost and low-lying mist, and dawn had yet to break. Five wagons and the brake van were detached from the rest of the train when a draw hook failed and came to a stop a short distance outside Shrivenham station in Wiltshire.

Unfortunately, neither the signalman at the Shrivenham box nor a colleague located in the box at Ashbury Crossing, a little way down the track to the east, noticed the dangerous blockage on the line. Both also failed to note that the coal train had passed and did not have any rear warning lights. These were on the stationary brake van.

Both gave the all-clear to the sleeper express from Penzance, which was following closely behind the coal train. However, disaster could still have been avoided if the guard on the coal train had gone back down the track waving his red light to indicate the blockage. He

Above: One of the carriages of the sleeper express wrecked in the collision at Shrivenham, Wiltshire.

Above: The aftermath of the incident at Shrivenham. Here, police and rail officials examine the remains of the Penzance sleeper express.

did not do so, and the high-speed impact became inevitable. Shortly before 0530 hours, the sleeper ran into the halted brake van and coal wagons at a speed of approximately 50mph (80km/h), killing the driver of the express and one of its passengers. It was a remarkably small number of fatalities given the speed at which the crash took place.

Both the express's driver and fireman had spotted the three red warning lights on the back and sides of the coal train's detached and stationary brake van and the driver applied his brakes, but was unable to stop before hitting the obstruction.

The brake van and three of the loaded coal wagons were smashed in the impact and the two other wagons were propelled some considerable distance farther down the track. The locomotive pulling the sleeper,

'King William III', rode over the wreckage and was sent crashing on to its righthand side. Its lead carriage, containing 34 passengers, suffered varying degrees of damage.

The front half was comparatively unscathed, but five of its rear compartments were destroyed. Most of the 10 people severely injured in the collision were found in this section, and the only passenger fatality, a woman, was also discovered here.

The second carriage of the express was also completely destroyed, but luckily it was empty at the time of the crash. The driver of the express locomotive, E Starr, was badly injured in the collision and rescuers took several hours to free him, but he later died from his injuries. The fireman of the sleeper escaped with relatively minor injuries.

WINSFORD, ENGLAND

APRIL 17, 1948

Left: Rail engineers and investigators attend the site of the Winsford crash, which involved a pair of trains heading for London's Euston station from Glasgow.

This collision just north of Winsford Junction station, part of the British state-owned network's London Midland Region, was brought about by the actions of an irresponsible passenger and an error by a British Railways' official. Their unfortunate actions caused an accident that left 24 dead and nearly 20 injured.

On the evening of April 17, an express from Glasgow in central Scotland bound for London's Euston station was brought to an unscheduled halt by a British soldier who pulled an emergency communications cord in one of his carriage's toilets. Almost unbelievably, he did this not because he was in any personal difficulty, but because he wanted to reach home as quickly as possible. Rather than travel a little farther down to Crewe station, change to another train there, and then head back to his home station, he halted the London-bound express with the intention of jumping off.

Meanwhile, at the Winsford signal box the British Rail employee on duty there mistakenly believed that he had seen the Glasgow-London express go by some

time earlier and, on this false assumption, allowed a following postal train, also from Glasgow, to continue on its way south to the capital. His 'train out of section' message to the postal train sealed the fate of the stationary Glasgow-London express ahead and its many passengers.

Back at the stationary express, which had been held up for a little less than 20 minutes by the soldier's pulling of the communication cord, a guard had gathered up his red warning lantern, left the train at the rear, and set off back down the track to warn any following traffic on the same line that his express was waiting to proceed after its unscheduled halt.

The guard had walked about 400 yards (370m) from the Glasgow-London express when he spotted the advancing postal train in the near distance. By waving his red warning light as laid out in safety manuals, he was able to slow the on-coming postal train, but the reduction in its speed was insufficient over such a short distance to bring the train to an emergency stop and prevent a fatal rear-end collision with the stopped express. Moments later, the crash occurred. It was a

Left: *As a crowd of spectators looks on, heavy lifting equipment is brought up to remove the remains of the two trains smashed in the incident at Winsford.*

Right: *The engine of the post train from Glasgow lies embedded in the wreckage of one of the halted express's rear carriages.*

little after midnight. The last carriage on the Glasgow-London express was totally destroyed in the violent smash, and the adjacent carriage was also badly damaged. Both contained several passengers.

In the subsequent enquiry, it was stated that the Glasgow-London express's guard might have prevented the accident if he had been quicker in leaving his train after the cord had been pulled by the soldier and then moved farther down the track, thereby giving the second train a greater distance to come to a complete halt. However, it was clearly stated that the wanton foolishness of the off-duty soldier and the mistake of the Winsford Junction signalman were the prime causes behind the fatal collision.

ROCKVILLE CENTER, NEW YORK STATE, USA

FEBRUARY 17, 1950

This incident on Long Island resulted in the deaths of 31 commuters. Rockville Center was undergoing major engineering work at the time of the collision. Railroad workers were separating the levels of the up and down tracks, but the only way to accommodate existing traffic during the construction period was to run trains on a single section of track for a short distance. Automatic signals were placed at each end of the single-track section and decisions on train priority were the responsibility of Rockville Center station.

The collision occurred shortly after 2230 hours when a commuter train travelling to New York from Babylon was given right of way on the temporary section of track by those on duty at Rockville Center. Signals were switched to halt any train moving in the opposite direction from entering the stretch of single track. The journey progressed smoothly enough until the Babylon-New York train was on the point of leaving the single-track and returning to its own line.

At this moment, however, it was struck by a train also packed with passengers, many returning home after a night out, which had gone through the protecting signals. Both drivers survived the 50mph (80km/h) collision, which saw the two trains strike each other at a slight angle, because their cabs were positioned away from the point of impact, but commuters on both trains died when the lefthand sides of the carriages they occupied were crushed.

An enquiry revealed that the driver of the train responsible for the incident had seen the stop signal and heard a warning buzzer sound in his cab, but had suffered a momentary loss of consciousness due to a medical condition. His version of events was accepted by the investigators.

Below: The scene at Rockville Center, New York State, shortly after the fatal impact between two trains. One of the injured is taken out by stretcher while rescue workers try to free the trapped.

RICHMOND HILL, NEW YORK STATE, USA

NOVEMBER 22, 1950

Collisions at night are not an uncommon phenomenon on the world's railroads, as this incident which resulted in 79 deaths and 352 injured confirms. The crash in question involved a pair of 12-car electric trains. One was travelling from Penn station in New York to Hampstead station when a signal in the vicinity of the town of Jamaica indicated that it should reduce speed. However, when given the go-ahead to proceed as normal, the train's brake would not release fully.

The train shuddered to a halt because of the braking fault and, as the regulations demanded, the conductor disembarked with a warning lantern to keep watch at the rear of the train. Because the signal system in use on this section of track did not permit any halted train

getting under way to travel at more than 15mph (24km/h) when given the 'stop and proceed' signal until the next clear signal was seen, the conductor did not move any great distance down the track from his train. He expected that any following train would be obeying the same 15mph (24km/h) rule and would not, therefore, require as great a stopping distance as if it was moving at a much higher speed. It was to be an unfortunate but understandable miscalculation.

The conductor soon returned to the stopped train when he heard the driver attempting to move off. However, the train remained stationary because of the problem with its braking system. Moments later, the conductor had little time to do more than wave his red lantern in urgent warning as a second train loomed out of the darkness, advancing at high speed. Unable to

Below: A pair of cranes begin to gently lift one of the coaches crushed by the collision at Richmond Hill. At this stage, a number of victims were still trapped in the wreckage.

brake in the available distance. It ploughed into the stationary train, driving it forward by some 25 yards (23m) and causing multiple casualties among the passengers on both trains.

It was later revealed that the second train had also received a 15mph (24km/h) 'stop and proceed' signal. Its driver had followed the standard procedure correctly but then gradually picked up speed as he advanced. It was discovered that the second train was moving at 35mph (65km/h) when its driver attempted to engage his locomotive's emergency brake in a futile attempt to prevent the accident from occurring.

The driver in this following train was killed in the accident and investigators were never able to fully explain the reasons behind the increase in speed of the following locomotive that sealed the fate of the stationary train in front.

It was suggested that the second driver had misinterpreted the clear signal that should have allowed the stationary train in front of him to proceed as normal had it been able. He may have thought that it was directed at him, not the train in front, and, therefore, allowed him to increase his speed to normal, thereby setting in motion the chain of events that led to the collision between the two.

Above: *Rescue workers continue the grim task of removing the living and dead from the remains of one of the coaches smashed in the collision.*

Left: *Doctors and emergency crews begin the emotionally draining task of recovering bodies from the tangled wreckage of one of the two trains.*

HARROW AND WEALDSTONE, ENGLAND

OCTOBER 8, 1952

Below: Rescue workers aided by heavy equipment struggle to search through the tangle of wreckage created by the three-train smash at Harrow and Wealdstone station in early October 1952.

This collision remains one of the worst incidents ever to have taken place on the British railroad network. The crash between a packed morning commuter train on its way from Tring in Hertfordshire to London's Euston station, an overnight sleeper train from Perth in Scotland to London, and a twin-locomotive express running from Liverpool to Euston left 112 people dead and over 150 injured, many seriously.

The commuter train had been waiting at Harrow and Wealdstone station in north London for about a minute when it was struck in the rear with massive force by the sleeper train from Scotland. The impact sent wreckage flying on to the line that carried the Liverpool-Euston express, which careered into the obstruction just a few seconds later. The express's two locomotives were travelling at such high speed that they mounted one of the station's platforms, blocking the local electric line. Sixteen carriages suffered massive damage; many of them were reduced to an unrecognizable tangle.

The driver of the Perth-London sleeper was subsequently blamed for the disaster as it was stated that he failed to heed signal instructions. His 11-coach train, pulled by the 'City of Glasgow', a 'Princess Coronation' class locomotive, was more than 30 minutes behind schedule, partly due to fog, when the incident

Above: The shattered body of a locomotive involved in the disaster. Despite serious damage, one of them, the 'City of Glasgow', was repaired and put back into service.

notice or act on the warnings and continued at speed toward Harrow and Wealdstone.

Shortly before the arrival of the Perth train, the Tring-London passenger train, consisting of eight carriages, had been switched from the slow line to the fast line just north of the station by a signalman as usual, prior to reaching the station's platform. Consequently, the fast line's signals were in the danger or caution position but were ignored. The driver of the 'City of Glasgow' braked at the last moment but the collision could not be avoided. After the first collision had taken place and wreckage blocked the path of the Liverpool-Euston train, the second devastating impact was an absolute certainty.

The local emergency services were swamped by the scale of the accident and their systems for dealing with a crash of this magnitude were shown to be inadequate, despite their best efforts. However, US military personnel drafted in from nearby bases implemented the triage system of assessing casualties on the basis of the extent of their injuries and did much to prevent an even heavier loss of life. The system was subsequently adopted by the British emergency services. The tragedy at Harrow and Wealdstone also provided further impetus for the introduction of the automatic warning system, which sounds a siren in a driver's cab when his train approaches a signal showing caution.

occurred, but conditions at Harrow and Wealdstone station were fairly clear. A signalman spotted the 'City of Glasgow' approaching when it was some 600 yards (554m) from his box and had time to lay down stop detonators on the track by pulling the relevant lever. For reasons never fully explained, the driver failed to

Right: Once the casualties had been evacuated, it was essential that the station was opened as quickly as possible. Here, rail workers and firemen prepare to remove a wrecked carriage.

CONNEAUT, OHIO, USA

MARCH 27, 1953

Below: One of the locomotives derailed in the Conneaut collision lies on its side. One of the pipes that played a key part in the smash can be seen in the bottom left section of the photograph.

This incident was brought about by the failure of railroad inspectors to check the fastenings that held a cargo of large pipes in place. These had, in fact, been loaded incorrectly at their point of origin – a steel works in Aliquippa, Pennsylvania. Some of the pipes were placed above the sides of the wagons on to which they were loaded. These two errors led to 21 deaths in the subsequent collision which involved three trains.

The pipes, each over a foot (30cm) in diameter and more than 30 feet (9.2m) long, had been placed on wagons pulled by a freight train heading eastward along a mainline consisting of four tracks. As the freight train was making its journey, movements were sufficiently great to further loosen the fastenings and one of the large pipes worked its way free, becoming lodged between a wagon and an adjacent track.

The impact of the pipe as it was dragged along led to the second track being pushed out of position by approximately 18 inches (45cm). A westbound train travelling in excess of 70mph (112km/h) was derailed by the distorted track as it was passing the freight train into which it collided, scattering wreckage across the rail lines. This wreckage on the track sealed the fate of the eastbound 'Southwestern Limited', also travelling at 70mph (112km/h). With the exception of its last three carriages, the 'Southwestern Limited' was derailed. Seven of the passenger coaches from the two passenger trains were totally destroyed in the incident.

HARMELEN, NETHERLANDS

JANUARY 8, 1962

This mid-winter incident involved an express travelling between Utrecht and Rotterdam and a local commuter train working the eastbound track between Rotterdam and Amsterdam. Both trains were moving at high speed when the impact occurred and there was fog about. The incident took place just as the stopper was approaching the junction at Harmelen, a little to the east of Woerden. At this point, the track layout was such that trains travelling between Woerden and Amsterdam had to use a section of westbound track for a distance of approximately 25 yards (23m).

The head-on collision occurred on this short section of track. The express, which was carrying 900 commuters on their way back to work after the weekend break, smashed into the stopping train with considerable impact. Three of the stopper's coaches were destroyed, while six of the express's 11 coaches were also badly damaged. The carnage caused by the smash was such that rescue workers toiled throughout the day to sift through the twisted wreckage and help the dazed and injured survivors.

Responsibility for the crash was laid at the feet of the express's driver. He had missed one signal notifying him of the train ahead and only began to apply the brakes when he saw a stop signal registering danger. He was able to reduce speed from nearly 80mph (128km/h) to 65mph (104km/h), but could not prevent the collision in the stopping distance available to him. With 93 dead, this incident was one of the worst ever collisions experienced on the Dutch railway network. Subsequent recommendations included the introduction of more modern safety devices.

Above: A Dutch doctor (dressed in white coat) prepares to enter the remains of a passenger coach to give medical assistance to those injured at Harmelen.

SCHIEDAM, NETHERLANDS

MAY 4, 1976

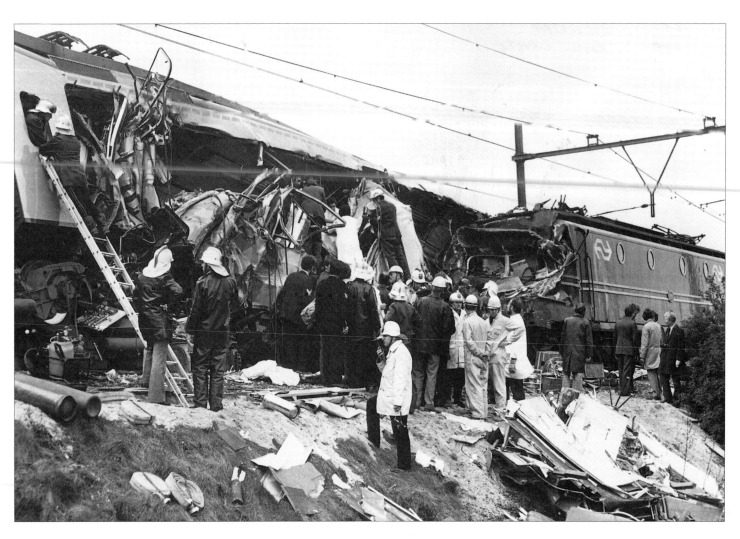

Above: The lead carriage of the stationary commuter train which was involved in the Schiedam crash. Most of the casualties in the collision were found here.

The crash at Harmelen in the Netherlands on January 8, 1962 heralded the introduction of an automatic train protection system, but by the time of this collision which left 24 passengers dead, only 25 percent of the Dutch railroad network had received the safety device. The incident at Schiedam in May 1976 hastened the widespread adoption of the system and a decade later some 60 percent of the network had received the device.

The collision at Schiedam began when the international 'Rhine Express' was delayed leaving the Hook of Holland, heading eastward on the righthand track. The train was switched to the lefthand track as it was nearing the Rotterdam-Den Haag line at Schiedam so that it could overtake a slower stopping train also travelling on the righthand track.

Most Dutch lines of the time had signals which permitted travel in either direction on a single track, so there should have been no difficulty in carrying out this simple switch. However, disaster struck when another passenger train heading westward on the lefthand track ignored stop signals and failed to halt before entering the section of line for the Hook of Holland. As the 'Rhine Express' electric locomotive passed the now stationary stopping train on the righthand track, it was hit head-on by the second local passenger train also operating on the lefthand track.

Consequently, all three trains became involved in the fatal collision. The first passenger coach of the westbound train was crushed by the impact between the two trains heading in opposing directions on the adjacent track. It was here that the greatest number of casualties occurred.

LEBUS, EAST GERMANY

JUNE 27, 1977

Before the reunification of East and West Germany in the late 1980s, information on train collisions or other rail accidents in the communist German Democratic Republic was difficult to find because of the state's strict control of the media. However, this incident was somewhat unusual in that western journalists were allowed to visit the site of the crash later during the same day. Their reports indicated that the smash was the product of faulty routing.

Early on the morning of June 27, a steam-locomotive express was heading to the port of Stralsund on the Baltic coast from the town of Zittau on the border with Czechoslovakia, a distance of approximately 300 miles (480km). The collision took place close to the border with Poland, and the northbound express hit a diesel freight train while travelling at speed.

The violence of the high-speed impact initiated a series of ferocious fires that totally gutted the two locomotives involved and blocked the tracks in the vicinity of the crash with burning wreckage for several hours. The dangerous conflagration was finally brought under control by the East German emergency services. Nevertheless, the remains of the two badly damaged trains were still smouldering when the contingent of foreign journalists arrived on the scene to cover the story.

Subsequent investigations by the East German authorities revealed that the Stralsund-bound express had been incorrectly routed on to the wrong line as it was about to pass through the junction at Bossen, thereby ensuring that it would collide with the on-coming freight train. This seemingly simple error in switching procedure led to the death of 29 people on the two trains.

Below: The wreck of the passenger train involved in the collision near Lebus station gives some indication of the ferocity of the impact and the subsequent fire.

ARGENTON-SUR-CREUSE, FRANCE

AUGUST 31, 1985

The summer of 1985 was not a good time for the French national railroads. In the space of two months, three serious incidents shook the faith of the French public in their state transport system and led to the resignation of the president of the railroads. This incident, which left 43 people dead and a further 38 injured, involved a train scheduled to make the southerly journey from Paris to Port Bou on the country's Mediterranean coast close to the Spanish frontier and a postal train from Brive, south of Limoges, to Paris.

The crash took place at night on a section of track that was being overhauled. The driver of the Paris-Port Bou train received a warning in his cab to reduce his speed as he approached the section of track being upgraded. His train, which was advancing at nearly 90mph (144km/h), braked to 65mph (104km/h) after receiving the normal warning regarding the curve in the track. However, a second warning to reduce his speed to 20mph (32km/h) was misinterpreted. The driver believed this second warning to be nothing more than a reminder to keep to the 65mph (104km/h) limit on the curved section. Consequently, he continued south at this regulation speed, only applying the brakes when the danger of negotiating the curve became clear at the last moment.

His failure to recognize the second order to reduce speed over the track led to the derailment of the train. The driver, sensing danger at the approach of the Brive-Paris train, then attempted to warn his opposite number by flashing his lights. His frantic, last-minute efforts to prevent a collision were to no avail, however. The driver of the post train was unable to brake in the short distance available to him and smashed into the derailment at high speed.

Right: Rescuers crowd around the two trains involved in the incident at Argenton-sur-Creuse in central France. A derailment caused by excessive speed was followed by a collision.

PUBAIL, BANGLADESH

JANUARY 15, 1989

Right: Heavy lift equipment is used to remove parts of one of the derailed carriages from the track following the incident at Pubail which left over 150 dead and many hundreds injured.

There have been many catastrophic train incidents on the Indian sub-continent, but this collision must rate as one of the worst. In a matter of moments, 170 travellers were killed and over 400 injured, many seriously. The collision involved an express service from Chittagong, a major Bangladeshi port situated on the Bay of Bengal, and a post train heading north. Both trains were packed with commuters, who filled the seats and passage-ways, and perched on the carriage roofs. Many of the 2000 passengers on the train were religious pilgrims heading for Tongi to attend the largest annual gathering of Muslims outside Mecca in Saudi Arabia.

The collision caused carnage. Derailed carriages were overturned by the impact of the two trains and rolled down steep embankments into paddy fields adjacent to the tracks. Many of the passengers were crushed to death or suffered serious injuries as the carriages rolled over. Bangladeshi soldiers were rushed to the scene of the accident from a nearby camp, but their rescue efforts were hindered by the large crowds that had gathered to view the wreckage.

How then did the two trains and the passengers meet their fate? Investigators discovered that many staff employed by Bangladeshi Railways were not qualified to operate a signalling system that had been recently installed. Their lack of training had caused a collision that led to nearly 600 casualties.

Right: Passengers from a second train look down on the derailed carriages of one of the two trains involved in the collision at Pubail, 15 miles (24km) west of Dhaka, the country's capital.

SHIGARAKI, JAPAN

MAY 14, 1991

Above: The badly smashed remains of one of the two trains involved in the collision at Shigaraki. Crash investigators prepare to sift through the wreckage.

Japan's railroad network has not been immune to tragedies, but they have a reputation for being safety conscious and all major incidents are treated extremely seriously. Before this collision in the central region of the country, there had not been a rail disaster of such magnitude for nearly 30 years.

On November 9, 1963, the wreckage from a derailed goods train involved in a smash with a truck on a crossing was hit by two passenger trains travelling in opposite directions. The severity of this unusual incident near the city of Yokohama can be gauged from the extensive casualty list: over 160 passengers on the crowded commuter trains were killed and 120 others were injured.

The May 1991 crash, however, produced an even greater roll of casualties. A pair of diesel trains filled with commuters struck each other head-on while travelling at some speed. The impact crushed the drivers' cabs and smashed many carriages, some well beyond feasible repair. Track was torn up for a considerable distance and the trains derailed.

When rescue workers reached the scene, they were confronted by twisted wreckage and hundreds of dead and injured. As the chaos gave way to order, lists of fatalities and those injured were drawn up. The total were, respectively, 40 and 400. Although the number of dead was just a quarter of those that died in 1963, the number of injured was over three times as great, making this one of the most catastrophic events in the recent history of Japan's railroads.

KISSIMMEE, FLORIDA, USA

NOVEMBER 26, 1993

Most railroad collisions involve two or more trains coming into violent contact because of human error or a systems failure often involving signals or some other mechanical device. However, several disasters have been brought about by a train colliding with an object, such as a rock or a piece of piping, placed on the track, either deliberately as an act of wanton vandalism or inadvertently, as in the case of a truck or tractor stalling at a crossing point.

This incident just outside Kissimmee falls into the latter category. Although there were no fatalities in this serious smash, the train in question, Amtrak's prestigious 'Silver Meteor', travelling from Tampa to New York, was severely damaged in the collision and an estimated 80 of the train's 103 passengers were injured.

The late November incident began as Amtrak's 'Silver Meteor' was approaching Kissimmee. Unbeknown to the train's driver, a massive electric turbine was stranded across his path and unable to advance or retreat. There was little the driver could do to avoid a collision given such a short warning of the danger ahead and the 'Silver Meteor' smashed into the turbine.

The train was derailed and its carriages suffered serious damaged. The turbine was mangled and thrown off its transporter, and a section of track was badly twisted. Emergency services responded to the incident quickly, but the wreckage strewn about took some time to clear.

Right: The remains of the 'Silver Meteor' are strewn on either side of the track at Kissimmee, Florida, after its violent collision with a large generator in late November 1993.

HUMAN ERROR

Workers on the world's rail networks, especially the crews that operate their trains and the staff who run stations and signal boxes, are by and large well-trained and highly motivated, taking great care and having pride in their jobs. Most are equally aware that they shoulder great responsibilities, not least to the thousands of passengers who are in their charge each day.

However, they are not supermen and women, and many accidents have been caused by rail employees. More often than not, their regrettable mistakes are caused by momentary lapses of concentration that can be explained by stress, tiredness brought about by excessive working hours, or a suddenly worsening medical condition. However, a handful of accidents have been caused by wilful neglect of duty or the deliberate failure to follow established procedures designed to ensure safe travel on rail networks.

Sometimes these accidents can be ascribed to the actions of an individual; on other occasions a number of rail workers have been involved. On a relatively rare number of instances, passengers themselves have initiated a series of events that have led to disaster, apparently oblivious to the dangers inherent in their actions. Investigators trying to uncover the causes of an accident may often seemingly attempt to lay the blame on a particular individual on the flimsiest of evidence as some of the following accidents confirm, but on occasion it is man and not machinery or technology who is to blame for a rail tragedy.

Right: Against a backdrop of the wreckage of two West German passenger trains, rescue workers administer trackside first aid to one of those involved in this incident near Warngau, June 1975.

SHREWSBURY, ENGLAND

OCTOBER 15, 1907

The outcome of the investigation into this incident on the London and Northwest Railway caused considerable consternation among the system's drivers. They believed that the investigators' decision to blame the driver for the derailment of a 4-6-0 'Stephenson' engine and its carriages was far from watertight and that there may have been other explanations.

Below: The aftermath of the crash. The investigators put the blame on the driver but their evidence was far from convincing.

On the day in question, the train was approaching Shrewsbury station from the direction of Hadnall and was supposed to reduce speed to negotiate a steep bank down to Shrewsbury. As the train was running at night, its driver was meant to take notice of a speed reduction instruction. Nevertheless, the Shrewsbury-bound train did not make any reduction in its speed

and, as it reached a sharp curve in the track over a junction a little way outside the station, was derailed and thrown on to its side. Carriages and the engine were badly damaged, and 18 of those on board were killed. Among the dead were the crew of the engine and three sorters working for the Royal Mail.

Investigators were obviously unable to interview those whose direct involvement in the crash might have been able to shed some light on the matter, yet announced that the driver probably dozed off, thereby causing the incident.

It was clearly a far from complete analysis, and paved the way for considerable speculation in the press. Some newspapers suggested that the newness of the locomotive was responsible, but produced no evidence to support their claims.

QUINTINSHILL, SCOTLAND

MAY 22, 1915

Above: A news photograph taken a short time after the incident at Quintinshill gives a good indication of the effort required to re-open the lines blocked by the collision.

This accident in World War I remains the worst railroad accident to have occurred in Great Britain. The collision of several trains resulted in 277 deaths and caused a further 246 injuries; the two employees of Caledonian Railway found responsible for the crash were convicted of manslaughter and given prison sentences.

The tragedy at Quintinshill began with the late running of two overnight expresses that were heading from London's Euston station to Glasgow. A little after 0600 hours, a third train involved, a stopper from Carlisle, was given permission to head along the main intercity track in advance of the first express.

It was planned to take this Carlisle train off the main line at Quintinshill, which lay 10 miles (16km) to the north. Quintinshill had two side loops, one for use by up trains to London and one for down traffic to Scotland, on to which trains could be diverted from the main line. On the eve of the disaster, the down loop at the station was already holding a freight train heading

north, so it was decided to reverse the Carlisle train over to the up line.

It was at this point that the two signalmen enter the story. They had adopted an unofficial shift system that required the nightshift worker to use a separate piece of paper to record train movements after 0600 hours. These would then be entered into the official register by the dayshift signalmen, once he had arrived from Gretna Green Junction on a local stopping train. Shortly after the arrival of the Gretna train but before the replacement signalman had taken over from the nightshift worker, an empty coal train heading south was permitted to make for Quintinshill and wait on the up loop there because Carlisle station to the south could not cope with it due to the weight of traffic using the line there.

The nightshift signalman also accepted the first of the London-Scotland expresses into his zone of responsibility at this point and, while he was having a discussion with his replacement, was also informed that a special troop train was on its way south from

Larbert to Liverpool and could be expected to arrive at any moment.

The dayshift worker then took over the signal box which also contained two men from the trains occupying the loops and the fireman from the Gretna stopper, who, as regulations required, reported the presence of his train. The fireman returned to his train after a brief discussion in the signal box. One of the signalmen there then sent a signal which gave the all clear to trains on the up route.

The troop train was permitted to continue on the line and smashed into the local train, to be followed by the first of the London-Scotland expresses which smashed into the wreckage across the track. The violence of the collisions caused raging fires to break out that made many of the bodies unrecognizable.

Left: Rescuers deploy a lone fire hose to damp down the still-smouldering carriages on the morning after the collision. The ferocity of the fire can be gauged by the coach in the foreground.

Left: The dead and injured from the incident are gathered together in a field adjacent to the crash site. Many of the bodies were burnt beyond recognition.

GROSS-HERRINGEN, GERMANY

DECEMBER 24, 1935

Above: The scene at the bridge over the River Saale where the crash occurred. Some wreckage is strewn along the foot of the embankment and rescuers are clearing the track of obstructions.

This Christmas Eve incident involved a local train travelling from Erfurt to Leipzig and the two-engined Berlin-Basel express. Over 30 passengers were killed and 27 seriously injured because of the failure of the driver of the front locomotive of the express to heed two sets of warning signals. Casualties might have been even higher, but for the fact that one of the drivers of the express was able to slow his locomotive somewhat after he had noticed the second warning signal.

As the local train was leaving the junction at Gross-Herringen station and was crossing the main line on a bridge over the River Saale, it was struck on the side by the speeding express. Several of the carriages of the Erfurt-Leipzig train were crushed, one was thrown on top of one of the express's locomotives, and a goods van was left hanging off the bridge.

None of the local train's carriages fell into the River Saale, although initial reports suggested that a large piece of wreckage found in the river by emergency service workers was in fact a carriage. However, several bodies were later recovered from the icy waters and several more were reported missing so the final death toll may have been higher than the official statements of the time suggested. Passengers in the express received comparatively minor injuries as they were offered a measure of protection by the train's all-steel carriages which stood up to the violent impact surprisingly well.

NAPIERVILLE, ILLINOIS, US

APRIL 25, 1946

The causes of some disasters are not always clear cut as this incident shows. The driver of the train in question was indicted for manslaughter but the case was dropped because of insufficient evidence, yet there was no indication of any mechanical failure to explain the crash, even after signalling systems and the train itself were examined.

Below: Rescue crews use ladders to gain entry into one of the carriages damaged at Napierville, while colleagues remove one of the dead.

This crash, which left 45 passengers dead and 36 injured, began when the conductor of the westbound 'Advance Flyer' spotted an object thrown out from below his train. His driver then halted the train at the next station, Napierville, where the train's conductor dismounted and walked some 300 yards (276m) back down the track to watch for on-coming traffic. He immediately spotted the 'Exposition Flyer' approaching, which applied it's brakes, but hit the stationary 'Advance Flyer' at approximately 50mph (80km/h).

The impact was such that the second locomotive ploughed through the last carriage of the stopped train. The next carriage along suffered mild damage, but the following dining car was crushed into a U-shape, partly because of its lightweight construction.

Signalling in the area of the crash was examined for faults, but none was found, and the driver of the 'Exposition Flyer' did have sufficient warning to apply his emergency brakes, but there was no indication that he had done so. While there was no clear-cut evidence of human error, the lack of alternative explanations makes the Napierville accident worthy of inclusion in this section.

SOUTH CROYDON, ENGLAND

OCTOBER 24, 1947

This remains one of the most catastrophic accidents brought about by the negligence of a rail employee to take place on the British rail network. The incident happened on a foggy morning at the height of the rush hour as workers from southeast England were heading for their offices in London. Thirty-two people were killed and 183 injured in a collision near South Croydon that involved one train travelling between Tattenham Corner and London Bridge station and another also heading for London from Haywards Heath.

The accident was brought about by the Tattenham Corner train receiving an incorrect signal which indicated that the way ahead was clear. As it reached a speed of over 40mph (64km/h), it hit the back of the Haywards Heath train, which had reached a speed of 20mph (32km/h) shortly after it had been given the all-clear to continue its journey.

The crash was brought about by a misunderstanding between two signalmen operating somewhat antiquated equipment. Semaphore signals were still being used on this section of busy track, rather than the newer coloured lighting system. A signal for a train to proceed on its way given by one signalman could only be given if the signalman in the next box up the line accepted the signal.

Once the second worker had accepted the signal, a blocking lever could not be replaced until the train in question had activated a device on the track a short

Above: Over 30 people lost their lives in this collision at South Croydon brought about by a lack of understanding between two signalmen.

Right: A track-side view of some of the coaches that were destroyed in the two-train smash. Fog still blankets the crash site.

Below: A doctor and official emerge from beneath the remains of one of the carriages destroyed by the impact between the two trains.

distance from the signal. This rigid system of signals and blocks could be overruled by a signalman acting on his own initiative if one of the system's components failed for some reason, but the railroad authorities had laid down very strict procedures for tackling such unusual events.

On the day in question, a signalman manning the box at Purley Oaks forgot about the train from Haywards Heath, which had been waiting in the station for more than five minutes. His view was obscured by the thick fog that was blanketing the area, and which may have contributed to his misunderstanding of the situation. When he received a request from the next signalman down the line asking him if it was permissible for the Tattenham-London Bridge train to proceed, he thought that the Haywards Heath train had left the station, but mechanical failure in the signal system had prevented him from being informed of the fact. Consequently, he overrode the system without following the formal guidelines for dealing with such an event and gave his permission for the second train to proceed on its way.

Because of this serious breach of regulations, the second signalman was able to give the signal for the Tattenham-London Bridge train to continue its journey. A few moments later, the stationary Haywards Heath-London service was hit in the rear.

Perhaps due to luck or the hazardous conditions which forced trains to reduce their speeds, the incident was not as severe as might have been the case. Less than a third of those injured in the collision needed hospital care, and of these 58 only 41 had to be kept in for treatment. Nevertheless, 32 passengers had lost their lives at South Croydon because an employee failed to follow safety regulations.

WOODBRIDGE, NEW JERSEY, USA

FEBRUARY 6, 1951

The official enquiry by the New Jersey Board of Public Utility Commissioners that followed this crash that left 84 people dead and many injured blamed the incident on a driver who had exceeded the speed restrictions on a potentially dangerous section of track a little to the west of Woodbridge station in New Jersey. Early in the afternoon of February 6, a speed restriction was introduced on the section of track in question, where a length of the New Jersey turnpike was being overhauled and the track had been curved to allow the contractors to carry out their renovations. The driver of 'The Broker', a steam-powered commuter train packed with passengers because of a strike on the Jersey Central line, reached the 25mph (40km/h) restriction zone at a speed of 60mph (96km/h), thereby sealing the fate of the passengers.

The locomotive was able to pass the first section of temporarily curved track without any difficulty, but as it entered the second part of the curving section, its weight was thrown on to the wrong rail for negotiating

Below: An aerial view of the crash scene gives a good indication of the scale of the disaster. Two carriages lie on the edge of the bridge.

the curve. The locomotive was tipped over on to its righthand side, coming to rest on the top of the embankment along which it was travelling.

Seven of the all-steel carriages it was hauling were also derailed. Of these, four were scattered across the tracks, while one, the last of the seven, had been ripped open along the entire length of one side. Another coach came to rest jammed into a bridge, parts of which collapsed under the violence of the enormous impact.

The board of enquiry established that the driver had been aware of the speed restriction before he started the journey as he admitted to having read a special note to that effect posted by the railroad in his New Jersey depot. However, there was some question as to the precise section of track along the route to which the warning applied.

The route he was following, between Jersey City and Bay Head, made use of two different railroads with separate safety procedures. One section, that up to Perth Amboy, was run on tracks owned by the Pennsylvania Railroad, while the second, longer, stretch belonged to the New York and Long Branch. On the shorter stretch, speed restriction signals were not marked, but they were on the second.

Giving testimony at the subsequent board of enquiry, the driver claimed that he had been keeping watch for the relevant danger signals. As it was his first journey since the 25mph (40km/h) speed restriction at Woodbridge had come into force, he may have been lulled into a dangerously false sense of security on the early part of his journey and missed the subsequent danger signs.

Although the driver was held directly to blame for the accident by the board of enquiry, the lack of consistent safety regulations on the two sections of track may have contributed to the circumstances which led to the derailment of his train.

Below: Several floodlights illuminate the crash site as rescuers sift through the coaches in search of survivors.

Right: Two cranes attempt to right an overturned locomotive 48 hours after the disaster at Woodbridge.

NEWARK BAY, NEW JERSEY, USA

SEPTEMBER 15, 1958

The exact reasons for this crash were never fully identified, as three of the individuals probably best able to shed light on the incident, members of the crew of commuter train 3314 from Bay Head junction, died in the accident. The destruction of Train 3314 took place on the steel bridge that spanned Newark Bay. Built in 1926 to replace the original bridge which dated back to 1864, it consisted of a pair of twin-track high-level bridges that could be raised to permit the passage of river traffic.

There were stringent safety procedures in operation to regulate the movement of trains and the raising and lowering of the central spans. An automatic warning signal had been placed some 1500 yards (1385m) from the bridge and a second stop warning some 200 yards (185m) from the lift. As a further safety measure, a derailer had been built some 25 yards (23m) beyond the second signal. Normally, shipping had priority and the warning signals were against the trains when the bridge was raised for their passage.

On September 15, a freighter called for the bridge to be raised as Train 3314, consisting of two diesel locomotives pulling five steel carriages, was due to leave Elizabethport station, the last halt on the line before Newark bridge.

The train left Elizabethport and headed for the bridge, its crew seemingly paying no attention to the two warning signals which showed that it was being raised to permit the passage of river freight. The train then hit the derailer at an estimated speed of more than 40mph (64km/h), careered along the sleepers for a little way, and then the locomotives and the first two carriages they were hauling plunged through the gap created by raising the bridge and sank into the murky waters of Newark Bay.

Right: The second of the commuter train's three carriages to end up in Newark Bay is raised from its murky depths. A third coach was yet to be recovered from the scene when this photograph was taken.

Remarkably there were no passengers in the first carriage, but most of those in the second were drowned. The train's third passenger carriage, initially caught on the bridge's pier, later plunged into the river. Most of the passengers trapped in this carriage escaped, rescued by several small craft that had hurried to the crash scene.

Investigators' reports suggested that the accident may have been initiated by the different safety procedures that applied to different sections of the track in the vicinity of the bridge. Some 12 miles (19km) south of the bridge, along a section of the New York and Long Branch, there was a system which enforced a 20mph (32km/h) speed restriction once a locomotive had passed a signal indicating caution.

However, from that point to the bridge, no such safety measure was in place. It was also discovered that the usual practice was for the bridge to be raised not to its full extent, but rather just sufficiently to allow for the height of the passing vessel. If it had been raised to its full height, concrete counterweights would have been lowered sufficiently to block the track and might have prevented Train 3314 from plummeting into Newark Bay. Although raising and lowering the bridge to its full height several times a day would have been time consuming, it could have reduced the casualties.

Above: *A coach hangs from one of the bridge's piers with its forward portion hidden by the bay's waters.*

Left: *A wrecked carriage is brought to the surface by a huge floating crane.*

FREIBURG-IM-BREISGAU, WEST GERMANY

JULY 21, 1971

Below: Part of the 'Schweis Express' lies at the bottom of the embankment where it came to rest after it had left the tracks as the train's driver attempted to negotiate a curved section of track at high speed.

Although this incident that left 22 dead was in part the fault of the driver of the 'Schweis Express', it also highlighted certain short-comings in the way in which speed restriction signs were displayed throughout the rail network in the German Federal Republic. The accident occurred at night as the train was making its way from Basel in Switzerland to Copenhagen, the capital of Denmark, along the Rhine valley.

The driver attempted to negotiate a curve in the track at a speed close to 90mph (144km/h), more than twice the permitted rate, and the express left the track. Twelve carriages and the locomotive then crashed down a high embankment and smashing through an adjacent house. The two remaining coaches stayed on top of the embankment but slewed through 90 degrees to come to rest across both sets of tracks, blocking the stretch of line completely.

When the authorities investigated the Freiburg-im-Breisgau crash, they found it had remarkably similar characteristics to an event at Aitrang during the previous February. It soon became clear that the high speeds reached by the most modern trains coupled with night-time travel could lead drivers to miss the rather small signs showing that speed restrictions were in force. Changes were made to the safety system. Henceforth, the previous posts placed approximately every 1000 yards (923m) were superseded by larger trackside boards positioned no more than 250 yards (231m) apart. This procedure became standard throughout the West German rail network.

CHICAGO, ILLINOIS, USA

OCTOBER 30, 1972

A driver's failure to bring his 'Highliner' double-deck electric locomotive to a pre-planned halt at a local station in Chicago, even after he had been given specific instructions to do so by his conductor before setting out on this fatal journey on the Illinois Central Railroad, led to a violent collision between two trains that left 45 passengers dead and 330 injured, many seriously. The Chicago station in question, 27th Street, was known by railroad employees to be a regular 'flag stop', meaning that commuter trains would halt there on request. However, stops were made on a more frequent basis, chiefly for the benefit of the staff of a hospital who used the station during the rush hours.

On the late October day in question, the driver passed through the 27th Street station, ignoring his conductor's earlier request to stop the train to pick up passen-

Left: Firemen cut through the twisted metal of the Illinois Central Railroad train involved in the rear-end collision at Chicago's 27th Street station.

Left: The Michael Reese hospital where many of the injured were taken can be seen in the background of this photograph of the crash site. Many of its staff also used the service.

Below: Cutting equipment is deployed by the rescue services to slice through the twisted metal to gain entry into the carriages.

gers, but the 'Highliner', a unit only recently introduced into service by the railroad, was then brought to a sudden halt some 200 yards (185m) farther down the track once the error had been recognized by the train's crew. At this point, the commuter train was also more than 125 yards (115m) beyond an automatic safety signal that would have warned the crew of any potential danger farther back down the track.

The staff of the 'Highliner' then began slowly backing up their train with the intention of picking up any passengers that may have been waiting at 27th Street. This proved to be a serious error of judgment on their part. As the 'Highliner' went into reverse for the return journey, it suffered a violent rear-end collision with the following train, which was scheduled to pass though 27th Street without stopping. This struck the 'Highliner' at a speed of some 50mph (80km/h) and great damage was done to the rolling stock of both trains, particularly those closest to the point of impact.

The subsequent enquiry by the railroad also revealed that the driver of the second train was partly responsible for the closing speed at which the crash occurred. He had been given a yellow warning light at the previous signal which indicated that he was to reduce his speed to no more than 30mph (48km/h) before passing through 27th Street station.

This warning was not complied with, as the speed of the second train was nearly twice this when the collision happened, but the driver should still have been able to spot the reversing 'Highliner' as it made its way back to the station to pick up passengers and bring his locomotive to a safe halt well before the crash took place. Nevertheless, the chief cause of the smash was the failure of the 'Highliner's' crew to take adequate safety precautions before reversing their train into 27th Street station.

ZAGREB, YUGOSLAVIA

AUGUST 30, 1974

Above: Wreckage of the express from Belgrade to Dortmund lies scattered across the tracks at Zagreb station. Both its driver and his assistant received heavy prison terms for their part in the crash.

Two of those held responsible for this catastrophic derailment which left 153 passengers dead, the driver and his assistant, received prison sentences of 15 and eight years respectively. The length of their imprisonment reflected not only the long list of casualties but also the fact that they initially lied to the subsequent board of enquiry.

The disaster in the capital of the Croatian state of federal Yugoslavia involved an express making the long journey from Belgrade to Dortmund in West Germany. It was packed with native Yugoslavians returning to their places of work in West Germany after the summer holidays. The entire train was derailed when it attempted to take a curve on the approaches to Zagreb station at a speed of nearly 60mph (96km/h).

Regulations stated that the section should be negotiated at no more than 30mph (48km/h). It was also revealed that the driver and his assistant had ignored a stop signal shortly before the crash took place.

The locomotive's crew concocted a story that the express's brakes had failed at the crucial moment, but tests on them after the crash proved that they were in a perfect state of repair. The German authorities conducted experiments on rolling stock taken from a similar train to that involved in the Zagreb incident to also prove that the accident would not have taken place if the Yugoslavian crew had obeyed the speed restrictions. During their trial, the two Yugoslavians did tell the truth. They admitted falling asleep as they approached the curve outside Zagreb. Their tiredness and the derailment was caused by them working more than 300 hours in the previous month.

MOORGATE, ENGLAND

FEBRUARY 28, 1975

Below: The sad scene at London's Moorgate station following the crash there in February 1975. Members of the public look on as rescue workers comb through the crushed wreckage underground for survivors.

This crash at Moorgate station in London left 43 dead, including the driver of the train involved, and more than 70 members of the public injured. The investigation that followed the incident concluded that the deceased driver was responsible for the crash, although the precise reason for the failure to stop was never identified. An autopsy did not reveal any medical problem that could have led to him failing to stop and X-rays of bones showed that his hands were on the train's controls at the time of the smash. Equally puzzling was the fact that no mechanical problems with the train were ever found.

In the mid-1970s, Moorgate was a busy station, serving both London's Inner Circle tracks as well as being the end station in the capital for a self-contained commuter line stretching out to Drayton Park, less than three miles (4.8km) to the north. There had been long-standing plans to develop the line. Its initial construction was such that it could take mainline rolling stock, so that travellers from the more distant suburbs could reach the City of London on the Great Northern Railway.

The initial expansion scheme was, in fact, never completed and a second development plan in the early years of the 1960s also came to nothing. Consequently,

Right: Police, station staff, and rescue workers look on as one of the survivors of the Moorgate incident is transferred to hospital.

Below: The scene on the platform at Moorgate, showing the rear of the train. The front carriages were compressed to a fraction of their original length by the violence of the crash.

the rolling stock in use on the line at the time of the Moorgate incident was of considerable age.

On the morning of February 28, the driver in question brought his train, its six carriages packed with commuters, into platform nine at Moorgate. This end of the line was protected by an over-run at the end of the platform, which was some 70 feet (21m) long and ended with a 40-foot (12m) long sand-drag, designed to stop any overshooting train moving at relatively slow speeds before it collided with the end wall. However, the train was travelling at far too fast a pace for this safety measure to have little more than a minimal effect on the events which unfolded.

The train smashed into the end wall of the tunnel at such a high speed that the first pair of old carriages were crushed to less than half their normal length by the impact. The front half of the third carriage also suffered a similar amount of damage. It was in these front carriages that the majority of fatalities and injuries took place.

The mangled wreckage blocked the narrow and low underground tunnel, making the work of the rescue teams that rushed to the site all the more difficult. Such was the complex nature of the rescue that one passenger took more than 12 hours to be removed from the crash site, although he subsequently died from his injuries.

The accident at Moorgate station led to the introduction of a number of more modern safety devices on the network. Chief among these was a piece of equipment that came to be known as the 'Moorgate Control'. This is designed to stop a train automatically if a driver does not follow standard safety procedures for whatever reason.

WARNGAU/SCHAFTLACH, WEST GERMANY

JUNE 8, 1975

Left: The crumpled and twisted wreckage of the trains involved in the collision at Warngau brought about by errors made by three employees.

It is not only train drivers who can be responsible for accidents as this incident demonstrates. At fault were station staff at either end of the section of line on which the collision took place. The severity of their misconduct can be gauged by the fines levied against the three people held at fault. Two stationmasters were ordered to pay 5000 Deutschmarks each and a clerk 2000. All three were also given suspended jail sentences for their pivotal role in a smash that left 41 dead and 122 injured.

Rescue workers were somewhat hampered in their efforts because the incident took place at dusk and the roads surrounding the crash site were blocked by locals returning to Munich after spending the weekend in the region's mountain resorts. Congestion was so bad that helicopters were used to shuttle the most seriously injured to hospitals in the city.

The single-track section of line in question lay south of the city of Munich in southern Germany and the two passenger trains involved were packed with people returning home after enjoying a day out. The staff at the two stations made errors which allowed the trains to enter the single track stretch at the same time.

However, the press were critical of the fact that, according to the publicly available timetable, the two trains were scheduled to arrive simultaneously at opposite ends of the section. However, as was pointed out, the working timetable available to railroad employees was somewhat different and the fact of the same arrival times in the public timetable was not a contributing factor in the collision.

HINTON, ALBERTA, CANADA

FEBRUARY 8, 1986

Below: Sulphur and pipes lie scattered around the derailed and crushed remains of the trains involved in the crash. Intense heat from fires caused by the impact left much wreckage unrecognizable.

Twenty-nine people died in this collision, but the death toll could have been a lot higher given the immediate aftermath of the event. A pair of Canadian National trains were involved in the incident. One consisted of a large freight train pulling more than 100 wagons; the other was a passenger train. The crash was held to be the fault of the crew of the freight train who failed to wait in a siding located in the foothills of the Rocky mountains in western Alberta before the single-track section ahead of them was cleared of on-coming traffic.

The freight train continued its journey at high speed and smashed into the passenger train travelling in the opposite direction. So great was the closing speed of the two trains that both their locomotives exploded at the moment of impact. The leading coaches of the passenger train were left as a barely recognizable tangle of wreckage by the smash and their metal was melted and twisted by the subsequent fireball that engulfed them.

To make matters much worse for the rescue workers, the load of sulphur being carried by the freight train also caught fire, covering the immediate area with thick smoke and the poisonous fumes of sulphur dioxide. The more seriously injured passengers were evacuated by helicopter to the town of Hinton some 10 miles (16km) from the scene of the collision, while buses were driven to the accident site to take others to the city of Edmonton.

JAKARTA, INDONESIA

OCTOBER 19, 1987

Above: One of the factors behind the high casualty list in this disaster was the number of passengers who rode on the roofs and hung from the sides of the trains involved.

Indonesian railways have suffered many serious incidents since World War II. In April 1963, an express bound for Bandung from Jakarta left the track and one of its carriages was violently derailed and plunged into a ravine, leaving 37 dead. This incident echoed a similar event in 1959, when an express travelling to Bandung from Bandjar dropped into a ravine following an incident that was blamed on sabotage. Close to 100 people died and 14 were injured.

In November 1993, a pair of trains were involved in a head-on collision at Depok, a suburb of Jakarta. Both were badly damaged and there were a number of casualties. The impact was so severe that the leading part of each train was smashed into a near-vertical position which hampered the search for survivors. Severe though these three incidents were, they are comparatively small-scale events when compared with the disaster that overtook a pair of overcrowded commuter trains involved in a head-on collision which took place in one of the capital's southern suburbs.

It was not unusual for Indonesian trains to be overloaded. People were often to be found sitting on the roofs of carriages or hanging on to their sides or ends. On this occasion, it was to prove a fateful and lethal decision that contributed to a casualty list that totalled more than 150 dead and over 300 injured, many severely.

The impact was so violent that many carriages were crushed almost beyond recognition. Rescue services took many hours to sift through the wreckage in search

of survivors and the dead, and lighting had to be brought up to the crash site as night fell. Scores of troops from nearby army bases were rushed to the accident scene to help in the painstaking rescue work, but even with their invaluable help, the last surviving victims to be recovered from the wreckage, two young boys, were not brought out until nearly 20 hours after the crash.

Once the crash site had been cleared of casualties, the investigators were able to go about their business of searching for clues as to the cause of the collision. Initial reports from the crash scene suggested that the fatal impact had been brought about by a signalling error, but it was unclear if this malfunction was the product of a simple technical failure in the system's signalling apparatus, or whether it was caused by simple human error.

The Indonesian Ministry of Communications indicated that there would be a thorough investigation of the signalling system employed by the state's railways, but were unable to rule out human error as a possible cause of one of the country's worst accidents in recent memory.

Above: Troops and rescue workers pull victims from the wreckage of the two commuter trains involved in the Jakarta collision.

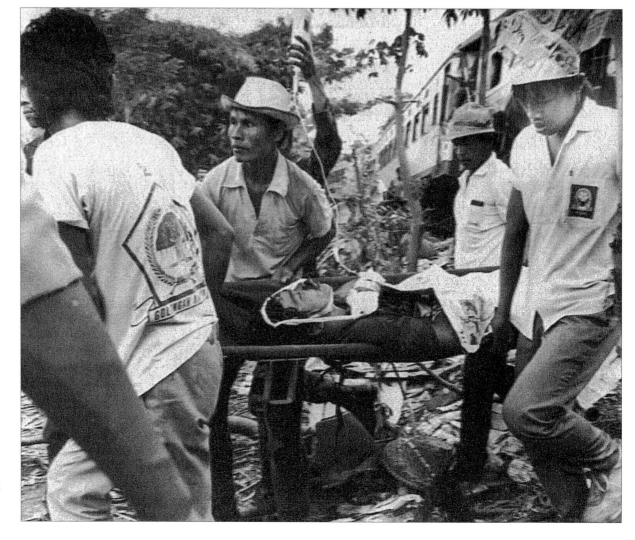

Right: Medical staff rush a severely injured victim away from the scene of the crash.

GARE DE LYON, PARIS, FRANCE

JUNE 27, 1988

The legal proceedings that followed this incident involving two trains on the Paris underground system proved highly controversial. The prosecuting attorney at the trial which began in late 1992 called for long sentences on conviction of charges of manslaughter to be imposed on a driver of the runaway train involved, a woman who had pulled a communication cord, a guard who had been late on duty the day of the crash, and a station supervisor who had apparently failed to order the evacuation of the public from the station.

The fatal collision involved a runaway electric-powered commuter train which hit a similar unit at the height of the French capital's evening rush hour. Nearly 60 passengers were killed and 32 serious injuries were also reported.

The woman who was later prosecuted apparently pulled the communication cord of the train from Melun as it was approaching Vert-de-Maisons, some five miles (8km) from the Gare de Lyon. She seemingly wanted to get home as quickly as possible and thought that the train was supposed to stop at her station, even though it was not scheduled to halt there. The driver had considerable difficulty resetting his train's brakes following the woman's intervention, but nevertheless

Above: The head of the crash investigation team visits the scene of the Gare de Lyon incident before the train wreckage was removed.

Right: Members of the French rescue services remove the dead and injured from the Gare de Lyon shortly after the crash.

Above: *Cutting
gear is prepared
to slice through
the wreckage left
by the crash so
that it can be
removed for
further study.*

he continued on his way despite the fact that they were apparently barely operable.

To make up for nearly 30 minutes of delays caused by the unscheduled stop, the driver increased speed to nearly 60mph (96km/h). On approaching the Gare de Lyon, he realized that his brakes were still faulty and, believing that a secondary system would not operate effectively because of the wet conditions, attempted to avert disaster by sending an emergency message to the Gare de Lyon. However, he was little more than a mile (1.6km)out when this message was transmitted.

Unfortunately, other incidents intervened to increase the severity of the accident. A guard at the Gare de Lyon was late in beginning his shift on a second train, one bound for Melun, which was waiting in the station on the track adjacent to the side wall of the tunnel. The runaway train smashed through its

leading coach, creating a tangle of wreckage which took rescue teams most of the night to search through and free trapped survivors and remove the bodies of the dead.

At the subsequent trial, the women and the supervisor were acquitted, but the driver received a prison sentence of four years and the guard was given a suspended sentence of two years. Following a nationwide strike by railroad employees who greatly resented the court's decision, the guard's sentence was reduced to two months. The driver was held in jail for six months before being freed.

Following the Gare de Lyon tragedy and two other accidents a few weeks later at the Gare de l'Est, also in Paris, and at Toulouse in the southwest of the country, various new safety measures were introduced on the French rail network.

PURLEY, ENGLAND

MARCH 4, 1989

This fatal rear-end crash took place on a Saturday afternoon in early spring and involved a four-carriage electric train travelling from Horsham to London's Victoria main line station and a second train of eight carriages making for the same destination that had originated in Littlehampton. The manner in which the collision occurred was easily established.

Below: An aerial view of the Purley crash site. The carriages were smashed as they rolled down the steep embankment, toppling trees as they turned over.

The Littlehampton train had run through warning signals as it approached Purley and careered into the Horsham train as it was transferring from the slow to the fast track after stopping at Purley station. Six of the Littlehampton train's carriages were knocked off the track and slid down the embankment in the collision, coming to rest close by the houses that lined the foot of the slope. Some of the local residents were lucky to

escape death or serious injury from the falling wreckage but five passengers were killed and over 80 injured in the disaster.

When rail investigators attempted to uncover the causes behind the accident, they took a close look at the signalling system in the area. It was up-to-date, having been installed little more than five years prior to the smash, but had been plagued with minor problems in the recent past. These were corrected at the time but it was not inconceivable that new faults could have developed in the interim.

However, the system was examined closely by crash investigators and no obvious faults were found. It was concluded that the driver in charge of the Littlehampton train had failed to pay attention to a warning signal outside Purley and cancelled the noise emanating from his automatic warning device.

The driver in question was granted limited immunity from prosecution on the understanding that he gave evidence before the board of enquiry, but was then charged with manslaughter and endangering public life, and went on trial at London's Central Criminal Court some 18 months after the accident. He pleaded guilty to the charges brought against him, receiving a sentence of 18 months in prison, with a year suspended. However, his sentence was later reduced on appeal following a public campaign against the severity of the court's decision.

The Purley collision also highlighted some failings of the existing automatic warning system fitted to train cabs and encouraged the introduction of an automatic train protection system which would stop a train even if a driver ignored its audible danger warning.

Some trains also began to be fitted with sophisticated recording devices similar to those used in aircraft so that investigators could study the sequence of events leading up to a crash and draw conclusions from the scientific evidence generated by these 'black box' recorders.

Right: One of the stricken carriages is carefully removed from the accident scene by a large crane.

Right: Police, firemen, and investigators prepare to begin their different tasks. The nearness of the wreckage to local houses clearly shows that an even severer accident was only narrowly avoided.

PINETOWN, SOUTH AFRICA

MARCH 8, 1994

Above: The accident at Pinetown left over 60 passengers dead and many more injured. Here, rescue workers and onlookers attend the scene of the derailment.

Accidents have been a feature on South Africa's usually safe railroad network since the earliest days of travel by train. Sometimes they have been relatively minor incidents with few serious casualties while others have led to many deaths. As is common, these disasters have been caused by many factors, but the one at Pinetown in early 1994 involved a derailment that led to more than 60 deaths and left many passengers nursing injuries. Initial newspaper figures suggested that over 200 of those on board the commuter train needed treatment following the accident.

The commuter train came off the tracks as it was negotiating a sharp curve in the vicinity of Durban in the state of Natal. Many of its carriages keeled over into the slope that backed on to the curve as the train's forward momentum switched their weight to the outside of the curve and thus shifted their centre of gravity too far over for them to return to an upright position before coming into close contact with the adjacent slope.

Although the list of casualties was awful enough, it could have been much greater if the train had been travelling on the adjacent track and the derailment had precipitated the packed carriages toppling into the fields immediately below.

South African crash and safety investigators studying the incident in great detail concluded that the derailment at Pinetown had been caused by the commuter train trying to negotiate the curved section of track at excessive speed.

STRUCTURAL FAILURE

This chapter looks at serious accidents caused by malfunctions within the various systems, both mechanical and human, that are or have been in use on the world's rail networks and usually ensure that passengers travel in safety. However, no system is perfect or immune to failure. Given the sophistication of much rail technology, such events are comparatively rare, but when they do occur the results can be catastrophic.

Signal systems, rails, and a wide range of faults associated with trains and rolling stock have produced the greater part of the accidents discussed here. Some were probably unavoidable, others might have been prevented by a measure of forethought, while others call into question the working practices that rail staff have been forced to adopt to improve efficiency. In some of these disasters, mechanical problems have been compounded by the failure of staff to react to the emergency in an appropriate manner, but in other cases they have performed to the best of their abilities and undoubtedly saved lives.

One element common to many of these crashes is that the main cause of the accident can seem, at least to the lay observer, an apparently trivial matter. A small fire, a tiny piece of broken rail, or an electrical fault have all played their part in these emergencies and have led to the death or serious injury of hundreds of passengers. The message is clear: constant vigilance, attention to detail, and regular maintenance are vital if disasters are to be avoided in the future.

Right: The interior of the Channel Tunnel following the November 1996 fire. The high temperatures generated by the conflagration were sufficient to melt the steel and concrete walls.

PARIS, FRANCE

AUGUST 10, 1903

This incident, which left 84 commuters dead, took place on the French capital's metro system and was caused by a mechanical fire. The Companie de Chemin de Fer Métropolitan de Paris's stock on Line Two of the system was powered by electricity, with the power control device situated in the cab at the front of each train and a power line linked the pair of motor cars located at each end of the train. On the evening in question, smoke began billowing from the power controller on Train 43 at the height of the rush hour.

Station staff reacted promptly, evacuating the passengers of the smoking train and calling for the next train to run into the station so that it could move the first to a place of relative safety. Passengers from the second train were also ordered to disembark, thereby adding to the crush on the platforms.

Initially, the intention was to run the damaged train into sidings at Belleville, but this proved impossible because of difficulties with points and it was decided to move the endangered train to the more distant Nation terminus station.

As this procedure was taking place, the leading wooden vehicle burst into flames just as the train entered Ménilmontant station. At the same moment, a following train entered the station at Couronnes. Staff here spotted the denser smoke from the burning train in front flooding out of the tunnel and attempted to get the hundreds of passengers out of the station.

Many refused to move, but a sudden failure in the lighting system induced panic on the crowded platforms. Dozens were killed in the ensuing crush; others escaped by walking back through the tunnel to Belleville station.

Left: French rescue workers struggle to reach the passengers trapped under ground following the fire caused by a train's electric system. Many passengers died because of smoke inhalation, while others were crushed to death.

FRANKFORD JUNCTION, PHILADELPHIA, USA

SEPTEMBER 6, 1943

Above: A body is recovered from the wreckage of the 'Congressional Limited' following the incident in northeast Philadelphia.

This catastrophe began in the leading dining car of the 'Congressional Limited' and was instigated by intense heat which led to the shearing off of part of an axle in contact with a bearing. The electric-powered express was pulling 16 carriages on this particular journey and it was packed with commuters enjoying the comforts on offer on board one of the railroad's most prestigious trains. The mechanical failure could not have happened at a more inopportune moment. The express, one of the most renowned working between Washington and New York, was just picking up speed after passing the slower section of track around Philadelphia. Its published travelling time between Washington and New York was based on an average speed of nearly 65mph (104km/h).

The fatal accident might still have been avoided, however. Some two miles (3.2km) from where the accident did occur, members of the crew of a locomotive shunting rolling stock in a siding spotted the burning axle and reported what they saw to a signal

box. Their desperate warning was just too late to save the 'Congressional Limited', as the axle then broke before safety measures to bring the train to a halt and evacuate the passengers could be implemented.

The sheared axle caused the dining car to derail and then collide with a trackside signal gantry that, because of the express's rising speed, sliced through the entire length of the packed dining car, leaving it mangled almost beyond recognition. The next carriage along was also wrecked by the gantry impact and several more were derailed. Rescue workers sifting through the smashed and derailed carriages found 79 passengers dead and more than 100 injured.

Concern was expressed over the mechanics of the dining car, which had been added to the train at the last minute to cope with the rush of weekend passengers, that began the disaster. It was one of only two carriages hauled by the express that day that did not

have a more advanced axle and bearing system. However, much of this speculation was rejected by the crash investigators. They stated that one of the more advanced coaches had experienced a similar, if less fatal, accident only a few months prior to the Frankford Junction incident and that the high death toll on the 'Congressional Limited' was not caused by the derailment itself but by the unfortunate collision with a substantial piece of trackside equipment – the signal gantry. Such an object had not been present in the derailment of the more modern carriage.

Commentators also noted that much of the criticism directed at the dining car was generated by individuals who had items of modern rail equipment to sell to the various railroad companies and that, consequently, their judgment may have been clouded by questions of economics rather than being based on issues of passenger safety.

RENNERT, NORTH CAROLINA, USA

DECEMBER 16, 1943

This collision, which left 74 dead and 54 injured, began when the southbound 'Tamiami Champion' shuddered to an unexpected halt. Two of its crew descended to the track and began to search for a cause. Between the train's second and third carriages, they spotted a disconnected brake hose and a broken coupling. As one of the crew initiated repairs, the second informed the train's driver to implement safety precautions to protect traffic on the northbound line. Unfortunately, this work was never completed. More importantly, however, no one had immediately spotted the real reason for the train's halt: the last three carriages had been derailed by a faulty rail.

Below: A large crane pulls apart two carriages involved in the accident at Rennert. Many of the casualties were US servicemen.

Two of these carriages, one of which was leaning over at an angle of 45 degrees, were partially blocking the northbound track. Their passengers, none with serious injuries, were evacuated. A crew member then informed the crew stationed at the front of the train – a distance of 450 yards (415m) – of the situation, but failed to ensure that they knew of the derailment.

Some 40 minutes after the derailment, the northbound 'Tamiami Champion' reached Rennert travelling at a speed of 85mph (136km/h). Its crew were unaware of the blockage and received a warning only moments before the impact. The collision left the northbound diesel and eight coaches derailed. All but one of the dead were travelling on the northbound train.

BOURNE END, ENGLAND

SEPTEMBER 30, 1945

Left: Sifting through the tangled mass of the Bourne End disaster brought about by a degree of confusion over a signal system which led to a violent derailment.

Below: A badly damaged engine involved in the incident is lifted gently from the scene of the accident.

This derailment in the first few weeks after the end of World War II highlighted the potential dangers associated with signal warning systems and the possible confusion that even a railway's most experienced drivers might face in interpreting them. On this occasion, an overnight express of the London, Midland and Scottish Railway bound for London's Euston station from Perth in Scotland was derailed when its driver failed to negotiate a section of track at the approved speed.

The incident at Bourne End began as the express was crossing over a section of track that linked the fast and slow lines. The switch from the express's usual fast track had been made necessary by weekend repair work on the up line to London. The driver should have been aware of this potential hazard as the details had been published in a fortnightly briefing document and circulated to all the railway's staff. There was a 20mph (32km/h) speed restriction in force along the section of

Above: This aerial view of the disaster site gives a good indication of the damage inflicted on both rolling stock and track at Bourne End.

track in the vicinity of the work, although a train could have crossed the point at double this speed and not suffered any undue consequences.

However, the Perth-London up express was travelling at 50mph (80km/h), too high a speed to prevent the fatal derailment. The 'Royal Scot' locomotive left the track with great momentum and crashed down to the bottom of the high embankment it was negotiating. It was followed by seven carriages which landed on top of the locomotive with considerable force. Five more of the express's carriages were also derailed and only three stayed on the line. The violence of the initial derailment and the subsequent drop down the embankment left 43 people dead and more than 120 injured.

Although the driver had clearly been travelling far too fast to prevent the accident, investigators suggested that his failure to reduce speed may have been the result of him failing to interpret confusing

signals correctly. Recently installed signals some way from the point where the express had to switch to the slow track should have given the driver ample warning of the danger ahead.

These were placed some 2600 yards (2400m) from the point at which the track switch was to be made. However, in other sections of track, a signal similar to that at Bourne End would have preceded a second signal, one giving a final warning of the hazard.

It was possible to argue that the driver had assumed that this second type of signalling system was in operation at Bourne End and that, consequently, he believed he had far more time to make the necessary reduction in speed than he actually had. In this case, driver error had been brought about by possible inconsistencies in a network's signalling policies. Investigators recommended a thorough overhaul of warning practices on the rail network.

CUSTOIAS, PORTUGAL

JULY 26, 1964

Below: One complete side of this carriage was torn away by the violence of the impact with the stone piers of a bridge.

There remain several questions to be answered about the direct cause of this crash which produced close to 100 fatalities and left 79 people seriously injured. The specifics of the incident are not in doubt, however. A weekend train was carrying large numbers of Portuguese day-trippers who were returning to their homes in Oporto after a pleasant day out at a local beach resort. The train was heading for the city's Trindade station and was grossly overloaded, carrying nearly three times its recommended number of passengers. Many passengers had pushed their way on to the train rather than wait for the next service to depart.

As it approached a curved section of track some three miles (4.8km) outside the city, the first of the diesel-powered railcar's coaches was derailed and the second then smashed into the stone supports of a viaduct that crossed the line at that point. Fortunately, a third coach was brought to a halt.

Rescue workers faced a difficult task in searching through the train and administering aid to the many casualties. They had to work at night in the confines of a steep-sided, narrow-bottomed cutting filled with wreckage. Vital equipment had to be lowered down the slopes by rope and the injured had to be carried out using improvised stretchers or were placed on the backs of the emergency services' staff for the painful haul to the top of the cutting.

Many of the injuries were so severe that there was a real danger that the supplies of blood available for transfusions might run out. A hurried call for fresh donors was answered by hundreds of people in the vicinity of the crash site.

Investigators later discovered that the train approached the curve at a speed of more than 60mph (96km/h), considerably in excess of the recommended safety limit on the section of track, and it was this that brought about the derailment. The local media reported that the accident had been caused by the parting of the train's couplings. Whether this was the case or not remains difficult to establish.

Normally, a sudden uncoupling will halt both halves of the train automatically. The rear part may have the momentum to nudge into the forward section, but not usually with sufficient momentum to cause anything worse than minor injuries. Alternatively, if a rear carriage is derailed, the lack of alignment between it and the carriage in front is usually sufficient to bring about a coupling failure.

Equally, this can lead to sideways movements in a carriage, making it highly liable to collision with track-side obstacles, such as a signal gantry, the walls of a cutting, or the supports of a bridge. This argument, if applied to the crash at Custoias, suggests that a derailment led to the uncoupling and not an uncoupling which led to the derailment.

Right: Rescuers mill around one of the coaches involved in the accident at Custoias. The train was packed with trippers returning home after a day at the seaside.

HITHER GREEN, ENGLAND

NOVEMBER 5, 1967

Left: A shattered coach, the one in which many of the fatalities occurred, is secured to a transporter before being removed from the site of the Hither Green accident.

This derailment took place because of a small section of broken rail on the main line running from the town of Hastings in Kent to London's Charing Cross station. The chief crash investigator concluded that the amount of maintenance carried out on the track was considerably less than was warranted on a busy line and contributed to the failure of the rail. On the Sunday evening in question, a packed diesel train approached Hither Green, south of London, at 70mph (112km/h) and was beginning to reduce speed to meet the 60mph (96km/h) restriction that began at the station.

As the train travelled over the fractured joint between two rails, only the front axle of the third carriage was derailed and the remainder of the service stayed on the track for a further 450 yards (415m). Here, however, much of the train that had not been effected by the initial problem was derailed when the original derailed coach reached a section of crossover track.

Many of the previously unaffected carriages were dragged off the track by the impact of the original derailed carriage with the crossover rails. Only the leading car remained on the track and four of the train's 11 units were thrown on to their sides. The list of casualties consisted of 49 dead and 78 injured, nearly 30 of these seriously.

The damage to the rail had occurred on a frequently busy section which was undergoing up-grading work. The work was seemingly progressing well and four months before the accident the speed limit in the area had been increased to 95mph (152km/h) for certain trains with more advanced bogies.

However, trains of the Hastings type were restricted to a maximum of 75mph (120km/h) because they had been modified by having their bogies made less flexible

to reduce the amount of swaying that took place at higher speeds and could prove dangerous in narrow tunnels.

Careful analysis of the fractured track and the surrounding area quickly suggested how the break could have happened. It was found to be located at a point where two short rails had been set between lengths of welded track. The bed of ballast which was supposed to support the two short rails was found to be insufficient to prevent movement particularly at the junction between the two and the passing of trains had led to the evolution of severe stress fractures.

These gave way, fracturing a triangular-shaped piece of rail and splitting a plate holding the two short rails together, as the Hastings train passed. To minimize the risk of similar accidents, the installation of continuously welded track was speeded up and the use of the short rails prohibited. These improvements came too late for the many casualties on the Hastings-Charing Cross train and their families.

Above: A carriage lies on its side following its violent derailment. The roof has been ripped off by the force of the accident.

Right: Working amid scattered wreckage and twisted track, heavy cranes begin the task of removing one of the train's smashed carriages.

RADEVORMWALD, WEST GERMANY
MAY 27, 1971

Structural failures can also involve the possible misinterpretation of a signal, particularly if the nature of that signal is open to debate. This signal problem led to a head-on crash between a diesel railcar and a freight train. The normal procedure was for the driver of the diesel to take his train off the main line, wait for the on-coming train to pass, and then rejoin the main line to continue his journey. On this occasion it appears that the driver of the diesel commuter service was scheduled to wait for the freight-carrier at Dahlerau, and only proceed once given the all-clear.

He did wait at Dahlerau as scheduled, but then saw a sign from the stationmaster there that gave him permission to carry on, taking his passengers, a party of schoolchildren returning home after an educational outing to Bremen, to their destination. He entered the single line of track ahead and was hit by the second train. Casualties among the passengers on the diesel train were heavy. Forty-six were killed and 25 suffered varying degrees of injury.

The list of casualties might have been much longer had the stationmaster, who was aware that the freight train had not passed, not attempted to attract the commuter train driver's attention by waving a red warning light and, when this failed to have any effect, rang the emergency services before the collision had taken place. Rescue services were able to reach the crash site in quick time.

Below: Stretchers are brought up to the wreck to remove the dead and injured from the train's coaches. Many of the casualties were teenage schoolchildren.

GRANVILLE, SYDNEY, AUSTRALIA

JANUARY 18, 1977

Above: An injured passenger is gently winched from one of the carriages damaged by the derailment and bridge collapse.

Australia's rail network has not been immune from rail disasters. There were several incidents in the early days of the network that led to a significant loss of life. Among these were a rear-end collision possibly brought about by brake failure or signalling errors at Braybrook Junction on April 20, 1908, which cost the lives of 44 and injured close to 150, and an incident between runaway rolling stock and an express at Murrulla in New South Wales on September 13, 1926, which left 27 dead and 46 injured.

However, this incident in Sydney, the vibrant capital of New South Wales, was a much more severe affair and caused a good deal of disquiet among the city's inhabitants. Some members of the public were so keen to find the guilty party that they sent the driver totally unjustifiable death threats. As events were to prove, he

played no part in the cause of the tragedy. A simple but costly mechanical failure was the reason behind one of Australia's worst accidents.

The incident involved a commuter train that was heading for Granville station located on the outskirts of the city. The train was travelling at 20mph (32km/h), a wholly acceptable rate on the section of track where the crash took place. However, a derailment occurred and several of the carriages left the track as the train was passing through a bridge that carried local traffic.

The violence of the derailment was sufficient to send two of the effected coaches crashing into the piers supporting the road bridge with such force that it collapsed on to the train. Steel and concrete smashed down on the carriages, crushing them, and causing the vast majority of the casualties. Several cars crossing the bridge at the moment of collapse also fell into the chasm, adding to the horror which unfolded.

Rescue workers faced a dangerous and complex task to search through the wreckage for survivors and bring out the many dead. They had to proceed cautiously to avoid any further collapse and were not able to complete their operation until the following evening. Heavy lifting equipment had to be ferried to the scene to help in clearing the wreckage.

Unfortunately, the rescue efforts were also hampered by the thousands of onlookers who had turned up to witness the disaster and who had to be controlled by hundreds of police so that the rescuers could continue their delicate work. By the end of the rescue, the emergency agencies could confirm that 83 commuters had been killed and over 200 injured.

Initial suspicion as to the cause of the crash focused on the driver. He, however, was found to be totally without blame by a board of inquiry. Its members identified the poor quality of the track near the bridge as being the cause of the derailment.

Below: The delicate and difficult task of clearing the track gets under way after the dead and injured had been taken from the crash site. Steel and concrete from the collapsed bridge also had to be removed.

Above: Several cranes have been positioned above the crash scene, ready to complete the task of removing the wreckage.

CLAPHAM JUNCTION, ENGLAND

DECEMBER 12, 1988

This early morning collision between two commuter trains packed with passengers heading back to work in London left 35 dead and nearly 70 suffering from serious injuries. A third train, one travelling down from London, then smashed into the wreckage caused by the initial smash. The incident began when the first train, travelling from Basingstoke in Hampshire to London's Waterloo station, was ordered to stop by a signal placed in a cutting a short distance to the west of Clapham Junction.

The signal turned from green to red as the train drew near and its driver applied the emergency brake. He then let the train coast to the next signal and reported the incident to the nearest signal box.

Left: Rescue workers toil in the narrow confines between the carriages of the trains involved in the crash at Clapham Junction. Dazed and injured passengers had to be lifted on to the embankment.

Above: A crane rips away a section from one of the crushed carriages as the process of clearing the line gets under way.

confronted by a difficult task. The trains contained some 1500 passengers, many of whom were trapped in their carriages by twisted steelwork and seats that had been ripped from their fittings. They also had to negotiate a ten-foot (3m) retaining wall at the side of the up track against which many of the wrecked carriages had come to rest. The last casualty could not be removed from the site until some five hours after the crash had occurred.

An official investigation team led by a top lawyer, Anthony Holden, quickly discovered that the crash had been caused by wiring mistakes made when a signal was overhauled some two weeks before the crash. As part of the modernization of this busy line, the Waterloo Area Resignalling Scheme was given the go-ahead in late 1984, but the work progressed slowly so as to cause as little disruption in services as possible. A maintenance worker installing new wiring in a signal box at Clapham Junction failed to carry out the proper procedures. Instead of shortening the old wire at one end and binding it in new insulating tape and isolating it at its live end, he simply pushed the live end out of the way.

A day before the accident, further upgrade work was being carried out and during the course of this, the first wire moved back to its original position and completed the original connection. The result was that the signal in question was kept at green even when there was a train farther up the track. It was discovered that safety levels had been allowed to decline over the years and that staff had been working overly long hours to complete the work in hand.

As he was telephoning, the Basingstoke-London train was hit in the rear by a train from the southwest of England travelling at 35mph (56km/h). It was at this point that the down train piled into the wreckage blocking the track. Emergency services rushed to the scene of the crash after being alerted by members of the public living nearby who had been stirred into action by the noise of the two collisions. They were

Right: Fire crews and emergency workers continue their search through the wreckage of the trains smashed in the incident at Claphan.

CHANNEL TUNNEL

NOVEMBER 18, 1996

Left: The section of the southerly Channel Tunnel with the badly damaged track and steel and concrete lining produced by the intense heat generated by the fire.

T his incident could not have happened at a more inopportune moment for those in charge of the Channel Tunnel link between England and France. Although the Eurotunnel company was winning over more passengers and freight from its rivals, it was still losing some £1 million per day. Any accident could potentially shake public confidence in the link and a closure of the system, however brief, might lead to freight returning to and staying with other forms of cross-Channel transport.

The cause of the fire which broke out on a freight-carrying Le Shuttle travelling in the more southerly of the link's two train tunnels remains to be discovered. However, speculation that it had been caused by an incendiary device thrown by a discontented French staff member outraged by the more than 650 redundancies announced for the link's Calais terminus seems to have been unjustified.

The normal procedure for dealing with a small fire would be for the driver to accelerate the train out of

the tunnel, but on the day in question, the fire developed so quickly that the freight train was brought to a halt within the tunnel so that its passengers could be evacuated into the central service tunnel that runs between the two main tunnels for carrying freight and passengers. This was accomplished with no little difficulty and some of those on board suffered from the inhalation of hot gases and smoke.

The rescue services had been trained to carry out their duties underground in the confines of the tunnel and eventually brought the fire under control. The locomotive itself was relatively undamaged, though badly covered with sooty deposits. However, several of the open-sided wagons used to carry large lorries – and their cargoes – were utterly destroyed. The heat of the fire in the confined space was sufficient to melt

Above: The Le Shuttle train involved in the Channel Tunnel incident lies in a siding at Coquelles, France. Its body is covered with smoke deposits from the fire.

Left: The twisted and melted remains of one of the open-sided cars used to transport goods vehicles under the Channel.

aluminium, and for a distance of approximately 800 yards (739m), the tunnel's concrete and steel walls suffered extreme damage. The track was also badly affected in the inferno.

It soon became clear that the impact of the fire was going to be felt for a longer period of time and cost a great deal more to repair than initial estimates suggested. Shortly after the incident, the Channel Tunnel Safety Authority in Calais took the decision to allow a severely restricted service to run along the undamaged northerly tunnel. Press reports suggested that the meeting, which lasted 14 hours, was acrimonious, but the authority finally granted Eurotunnel the right to run a maximum of six trains in each direction at 90-minute intervals once its ten-strong committee had been absolutely convinced that safety equipment,

especially fire-detection systems, was working effectively and efficiently.

Safety experts were also critical of the design of the cars used to transport freight under the Channel. The open-sided freight cars were a cheaper alternative than enclosed carriages. However, being open to the air they could not contain a fire once it had begun and, if the train was moving at speed, the passage of wind also moving at speed would fan the flames further.

While passenger services were severely disrupted by the fire, in which it should be noted that there were no fatalities, the operators of the system could take some comfort from the fact that the public returned to using the system once it had re-opened for business, and that the expected long-term drop in passenger revenue did not seemingly materialize.

Below: An investigator looks over one of the open cars damaged by heat and smoke.

PIACENZA, ITALY

JANUARY 12, 1997

This incident, which left several passengers dead and over 50 injured, involved the prestigious 'Pendolino', Italy's high-speed train, as it was heading from Milan in the north of the country to the capital Rome. The 'Pendolino' was scheduled to complete the journey in four hours, approximately half the time taken by regular express services. On the day of the crash, the tilting train was carrying well below its capacity, with only 150 passengers on board instead of its maximum of 900 travellers, and commentators suggested that the final casualty list could have been much higher if more people had boarded the 'Pendolino' in Milan.

The Piacenza incident raised issues regarding the state railway's intention to create a network of similar routes and trains through Italy. The ambitious plan had already been undermined to a degree when the chairman of the rail board had resigned his position after being arrested by the police the year before, charged with corruption and bribery with regard to the awarding of contracts for the proposed improvements.

The accident occurred at Piacenza, some 30 miles (48km) to the south of Milan. The train was negotiating a sharp curve as it was approaching Piacenza station and was suddenly and violently derailed. A number of the train's coaches were crushed and smashed, and

Below: The remains of some of the carriages involved in the derailment of the 'Pendolino' high speed express at Piacenza.

some ended on their sides. Among those on board the train was Francesco Cossiga, a former Italian president. He, unlike many of his fellow passengers, emerged unscathed. Local fire and rescue services were quick to attend the scene of the crash and got to work cutting through the wreckage strewn across the track in search of trapped survivors.

The immediate cause of the derailment was a matter of speculation in the press. Some passengers stated that the train was travelling at high speed as it approached the curve when they were interviewed shortly after the crash, but there was no indication that the driver was exceeding the speed limit on the section of track where the train was derailed.

Representatives of the rail unions had a different tale to tell. They intimated that the management of the state rail network had already been warned about the possibility of inadequate safety signalling in the area of the crash and that the authorities had allegedly paid no attention to their comments. Police and security services did, however, rule out the likelihood that the accident had been brought about by Italian terrorists looking to gain publicity for their cause through an attack on a prestige target.

Right: *An aerial view of the crash site gives a good indication of the ferocity of the derailment. There was considerable media speculation as to the cause of the accident.*

NATURAL DISASTERS

The world's rail networks have always witnessed incidents that cannot be blamed on faulty equipment, neglectful staff, or mechanical failure. Occasionally, train accidents have been caused by external events that have been completely beyond the control of the railways to anticipate or prevent. The natural world can be a potentially violent place and, as these disasters show, its forces can have lethal consequences for passengers and rail employees. High winds have caused structural failures, including the collapse of bridges, while rivers have become swollen with floodwaters and swept away tracks causing derailments, or have even crashed against trains themselves. Fires have led to the buckling of tracks and devastating explosions that have obliterated both train, passengers, and track.

These events are often so unusual, and thankfully extremely rare, that railway companies can do little except respond to an incident after it has taken place. Some structures, particularly bridges and embankments, need to be checked regularly for signs of damage by subsidence, water, and high winds, and they have to be built to tolerate certain expected stresses. However, not all natural events or the scale of their impact can be predicted or prepared for. In a few cases, the severity of an event is far in excess of what might be considered 'normal'. On these occasions, it is the speed of the response of the emergency services and rail employees that counts for most. Their prompt action is the only feasible way to limit the lethal impact of any natural disaster of unexpected magnitude.

Right: The catastrophic damage inflicted on one of the passenger carriages involved in the crash at Lewisham, England, between an express and a commuter train on December 4, 1957.

ELLIOT JUNCTION, SCOTLAND

DECEMBER 29, 1906

This accident took place in the depths of winter and was brought about by heavy snowstorms which affected the operation of a local signal system. Twenty-two people died in the subsequent collision between a local commuter train and an express.

The incident began when a southbound freight train was brought to a halt and split into two parts by a snowdrift. Its driver then decided to switch lines and return to Elliot Junction with the portion of the train still attached to his locomotive. Once there, he intended to switch back on to the southbound line, return to the stationary portion of the train and then recouple the two parts.

The manoeuvre took some time because of the conditions, and some of the freight wagons were derailed during recoupling. With one line closed because of the derailment, rail staff implemented single-line operating. However, heavy snow on telegraph wires put the signal system out of operation. By 1500 hours, the staff at Arbroath station, north of Elliot Junction, began getting their delayed trains under way.

First to leave was a local commuter train heading south and this was followed some 15 minutes later by an express from Arbroath that had been stuck at the station since the morning. Its driver was warned to keep his speed down on three separate occasions by rail staff, but failed to do so. He collided with the local passenger train at a speed of 30mph (48km/h) while it was halted at Elliot Junction waiting to be switched on to the single-track section so that it could pass the derailed freight train.

Below: Wreckage covers the tracks at Elliot Junction after the late December crash. Although the speed of the collision was not particularly high, the damage was extensive.

MODANE, FRANCE

DECEMBER 12, 1917

Above: Soldiers and engineers study the remains of the train involved in the Modane incident. So great was the loss of life that the French authorities tried to censor reports of the smash.

This accident, one of the worst in rail history, was a direct result of pressures put on the French system by World War I. The incident began with two trains of Italian rolling stock taking more than 1000 French troops home on leave for Christmas. After passing through the Mount Cenis tunnel, the two trains were coupled together at Modane so that they could negotiate a down gradient hauled by a single train. The train's driver, aware that the total weight of his 19 carriages was more than three times that permitted on the gradient, initially refused to undertake the operation.

Threatened with court martial, he finally agreed to proceed and set off at 6mph (9km/h). Despite applying hand brakes, the train quickly built up speed on the down gradient, partly because of the lack of grip caused by the wet rails. At a point where the line crossed the River Arc, the locomotive separated from the train after one of its bogies had become derailed. The leading coach was also derailed and came to rest against a retaining wall, where it was crushed by the remainder of the train.

Fire broke out and spread quickly, aided by the wooden rolling stock and the explosions of live ammunition that the soldiers were carrying home as souvenirs. Rescuers were kept at a distance from the wreckage because of the explosions. Over 540 soldiers were killed on the troop train, whose driver was later found not guilty of negligence by a court martial. News of the disaster was kept from the French public by the wartime censors.

WEESP, NETHERLANDS

SEPTEMBER 13, 1918

Above: The remains of the train derailed at Weesp lying at the foot of the embankment that gave way. The ship is loading casualties to take them to hospital.

This fatal derailment, which left 41 passengers dead and over 40 seriously injured, was brought about by heavy rains that weakened the structure of an embankment. On the day in question, an express train of 11 carriages was travelling along a high embankment prior to crossing the Merwede Canal. Unbeknown to the rail authorities a prolonged period of heavy rain had loosened the sand from which the embankment had been constructed.

As the train passed along the embankment, its vibrations were sufficient to set the saturated sand in motion. The train was derailed and its locomotive crashed into the steel girders of the canal bridge. Its wooden carriages were badly smashed as they tumbled down the embankment. However, the casualty list could have been much longer except for the prompt action of an army unit which rushed to the scene less than ten minutes after the derailment.

Other help for those injured was even closer at hand. A doctor, one of the train's passengers, was also able to administer immediate aid to the injured and vessels working on the canal transported many of the injured to hospital.

Investigators studying the crash site discovered that the sand embankment was far too steep and that a layer of clay had prevented the water from draining away, thereby permitting the sand to become saturated. The rail company was held responsible for the flawed construction of the embankment and ordered to compensate the passengers of the express.

LAGNY-POMPONNE, FRANCE

DECEMBER 23, 1933

This rear-end collision led to the death of 230 passengers and left 300 injured. The incident began with the late running of an express travelling from Paris to Nancy. It was delayed because of thick fog and was brought to a halt by adverse signals at Pomponne, a short distance outside Lagny. As it was moving off, it was hit by a second express, one travelling from Paris to Strasbourg, at 60mph (96km/h). The second train had also been delayed because of the fog and frost.

The Paris-Strasbourg express smashed its way along much of the Nancy train, which was packed with Christmas shoppers, and five of its carriages were battered beyond recognition. The vast majority of the casualties occurred in the Nancy express as the steel carriages of the Strasbourg train stood up to the impact remarkably well. Many of the injured were ferried back to Paris in those coaches that had not been derailed by the initial collision.

Charges were brought against those held responsible, including the driver of the Paris-Strasbourg express, and the trial began in December 1934. He was acquitted and the cases against other employees were also dropped when the court delivered its verdict in January 1935. It was acknowledged that he had been travelling far too fast given the foggy and frosty conditions, but that he may have missed stop and warning signals either because of the fog or because the signal mechanisms had been adversely affected by the frost.

Below: The crushed remains of the locomotive that hauled the Paris-Strasbourg express, one of the two trains wrecked in the crash at Lagny-Pomponne.

WAIOURU, NEW ZEALAND

DECEMBER 24, 1953

Below: The site of the crash which carried away the Wellington to Auckland express. Floodwaters caused by a volcanic eruption swept away the bridge seen here and the train plunged into the turbulent waters.

This accident must rank as one of the most unusual to have ever occurred in New Zealand as it was caused by the eruption of Mount Ruapehu, a volcano on the North Island. The Wellington to Auckland express was packed with passengers heading home to begin the Christmas festivities. The train passed through Waiouru on time and all seemed well.

Unbeknown to the express's passengers and crew a bridge ahead of them crossing the Whangaehu river was about to be washed away. The eruption of Mount Ruapehu had released the waters of the lake in the volcano's crater which proceeded to flow into the river valley through caves in a glacier. The massive volume of water travelling at high speed tore away the river banks, picking up debris as it headed for the bridge.

The waters swamped the bridge as the train approached, sweeping away its fourth pier and damaging the fifth. A motorist tried to raise the alarm before the train reached the bridge and the train's driver applied the brakes at the last moment but to no avail. The train roared on to the bridge and then plunged into the foaming waters along with six carriages.

Of the 285 people on the train, 134 survived the incident and of the 151 who died, 20 bodies were never recovered. Eight others were buried without being identified. So much force had been generated by the floodwaters that the remnants of one carriage were found more than five miles (8km) from the bridge.

KUURILA, FINLAND

MARCH 15, 1957

Above: Finnish emergency crews and investigators recover the dead from the Kuurila disaster site in the south of the country.

Many of the world's rail networks operate in the face of the worst types of weather imaginable and, as this incident indicates, no matter how efficient the system, those in charge are sometimes caught out by atrocious conditions. On this occasion, over 25 people died and 45 were injured in a collision in part brought about by a severe blizzard.

Two expresses travelling at high speed in opposite directions were making their way through the blizzard to their destinations. Some 80 miles (128km) north of the capital, Helsinki, they both entered a section of single-line track at the same time.

A little later, they collided violently, and the engine and leading carriages of each train were badly damaged due to the resulting derailment. Several had to be scrapped as they had been reduced to little more than shattered shells. The incident was the worst disaster the Finnish rail network had experienced since the end of World War II.

To make matters much worse for both the survivors and the rescue services, the remoteness of the crash site amid a dense pine forest covered in deep winter snow, delayed aid reaching the stricken trains and their passengers. Rescuers resorted to the use of skis and horse-drawn sleighs to reach the trains and remove some of the casualties.

LEWISHAM, ENGLAND

DECEMBER 4, 1957

Right: The aftermath of the collision at Lewisham. The list of casualties was all the greater because of the collapse of the bridge seen here on to passenger coaches.

Thick fog was a major factor in this incident which left 90 passengers dead and over 100 seriously injured. This rear-end collision involved a steam express travelling from Cannon Street station to Ramsgate in Kent and a local commuter train working between Charing Cross and Hayes.

The driver of the express ran through two warning signals without reducing speed and only began to decelerate when his fireman spotted a red light at close range. However, the express's speed was such that its driver, even though he applied the brakes, could not bring the train to a halt before it smashed into the stationary Charing Cross-Hayes train.

The 30mph (48km/h) impact was made more severe because the stationary train's driver had his brakes on full because he had come to a dead stop on an up gradient while waiting for a red signal to change once a train in front had moved off. The impact damaged many of

Left: One of the carriages from the Charing Cross to Hayes commuter train is removed from St John's station.

the Hayes train's ten carriages. The eighth carriage was smashed when the ninth was propelled into it by the express's impact.

The front section of the express also suffered severe damage when its front carriage was thrown into the locomotive's tender by the force generated by the rapid deceleration. Both the carriage and tender were thrown sideways and smashed into the central pillar of a bridge carrying the line between Nunhead and Lewisham. Some of the bridge's girders crashed down on to the wreckage below, completing the destruction of the lead carriage of the express and damaging the second and part of the third carriages.

One of the express's carriages had to be cut up before it could be removed from the scene and the line was closed for more than a week. But for the quick thinking of its crew, a third train could have been involved in the accident. It was about to cross the damaged bridge when they brought it to a very timely emergency halt.

The fog, which had been blanketing the area for most of the second half of the day, was identified as one of the main causes of the accident. The two trains involved had been experiencing delays during the evening rush hour out of London: the Cannon Street-Ramsgate service was more than 60 minutes behind schedule when disaster struck and the Charing Cross-Hayes train was 30 minutes late. Investigators also highlighted problems with the signal system in the area of the accident. Installed in the 1920s, they were visible at close range from the cabs of diesel and electric trains, but were obscured by the boilers of steam locomotives at similar distances.

The driver of the express should perhaps have made more effort to check for a warning signal himself or asked his fireman to do so. He was twice tried for manslaughter. The first jury did not reach a decision and the second saw the prosecution offer no evidence because of the driver's mental condition. He was therefore acquitted.

Below: The warped remnants of the bridge that crashed down on to the train below at Lewisham. Huge amounts of steel fell when the bridge collapsed.

ARZAMAS, SOVIET UNION

JUNE 4, 1988

Above: The deep crater left by the detonation of 100 tons of industrial explosives. Scores of civilians waiting at a level crossing were killed in the blast.

This dramatic incident on the Russian rail network took place at Arzamas, a town 250 miles (400km) to the east of Moscow, and left an estimated 100 dead and 200 injured.

The cause of this massive casualty list was a huge explosion that also produced enormous damage to facilities in the vicinity of the detonation. The incident began as a freight train was approaching a level crossing at Arzamas. For some reason, possibly the unstable nature of their cargo, three of its wagons exploded.

The three wagons contained a massive amount of explosives destined to be used by various industries. The violence of the unexpected detonation can be gauged by the fact that the wagons and much of the track were obliterated, and a crater some 80-feet (25m) deep was gouged out of the earth.

The violence of the spectacular explosion flattened an estimated 150 dwellings around the level crossing and left a further 250 buildings suffering from various degrees of damage. The headquarters of the local branch of the Communist Party, more than a mile (1.6km) from the crossing, had its windows smashed by the shock waves and a vital gas pipeline close to the track needed extensive repair.

The long list of casualties was in part due to the line of vehicles waiting to cross the level crossing once the freight train had gone by. Most of their passengers were killed in the first few seconds after the explosion, engulfed by the blast.

UFA, SOVIET UNION

JUNE 4, 1989

Many hundreds were killed or injured in this incident at Ufa, west of the Urals, which shocked many Russians and led to an officially sponsored day of national mourning. The incident had nothing whatsoever to do with the rail network itself but was brought about by a fracture in a natural gas pipeline lying a mile (1.6km) from the track.

Below: Wreckage, burnt and twisted by the high temperatures generated by exploding natural gas, stands testament to the scale of the disaster at Ufa.

Those responsible for overseeing the running of the pipeline spotted a drop in pressure caused by the leak but rather than investigate the cause they simply increased the flow of gas through the pipeline. The vast volume of escaping gas flowed over the countryside and much of it eventually settled in low-lying ground close to the rail tracks.

As two trains approached each other on the Trans-Siberian Railway, the highly volatile gas ignited. The explosion and subsequent fireball engulfed the trains and the flames, more than a mile (1.6km) wide, moved with such speed that they threw the two locomotives off their tracks and derailed several carriages. The destruction was not confined to the trains, however. Hundreds of trees were felled and many more were stripped of their bark and leaves.

Many of those who survived the fireball suffered severe burns. Rescue services were quick to respond to the emergency and many casualties were transferred to local hospitals by helicopter. Several of the worst injured were later flown to Moscow for treatment and a number of children were sent to specialist burns units in England.

MOBILE, ALABAMA, USA

SEPTEMBER 22, 1993

This accident involved Amtrak's prestigious 'Sunset Limited' and left dozens of passengers dead and many more injured. In the early hours of that fateful September day, the 'Sunset Limited' crashed, was wrecked by a violent explosion, and several of its carriages plunged into a muddy creek a short distance outside Mobile. The steel bridge on which the incident occurred had been severely weakened when one of its supporting piers had been rammed by a barge in dense fog earlier in the day.

The 'Sunset Limited' had entered service in April 1993 and was scheduled to make 50 halts on its trans-continental journey. The two-engined train was carrying many tourists, who were heading from Los Angeles for Miami in luxury carriages, when it approached the bridge over Cabot Bayou.

It was 0300 hours on a dark and foggy night. Because of the earlier collision involving the barge, the bridge could not support the train's weight and distorted tracks, also caused by the barge's collision brought about the 'Sunset Limited's' derailment.

The locomotive reached the bridge at a speed of 70mph (112km/h), and the derailment and collapse led to four cars, including two passenger carriages, plunging into the deep and murky waters of the alligator-infested bayou. Others were left hanging from the shattered remains of the bridge.

Passengers struggled to make their escape through smoke-filled carriages, while others clung to the carriages that had ended up in the creek. Some were able to swim to shore or form human chains in the water to help the weaker swimmers reach the safety of the banks.

Over 40 passengers died in the accident. Many were drowned in the carriages that plunged into the bayou when its murky waters poured through smashed windows. However, thanks to the outstanding efforts

Left: An aerial view of the Mobile crash site taken some hours after the luxury 'Sunset Limited' plunged into the Cabot Bayou. Rescuers had to cope with alligators.

Left: Salvage efforts are under way at the crash site. One carriage has been lifted on to a barge, while others remain where they came to rest.

of the emergency services and several brave passengers there were more than 150 survivors. The task of the rescuers was made all the more difficult by the remoteness of the crash site, the burning diesel fuel, and the poor visibility in the water. Those first on the scene had to work by the illumination provided by searchlights mounted on helicopters. It took time to get heavy equipment to the crash site because of the difficult conditions. As time passed, the rescue task became one of recovering the dead from the submerged wreckage rather than aiding the dazed and injured passengers.

Early investigations seemed to indicate that the barge's collision with the bridge had not only weakened its supports but had also distorted the track, but not sufficiently to trigger warning devices. The driver would not have had time to bring the train to a safe halt even if he had spotted the distorted track.

Left: A carriage hangs over Cabot Bayou following the crash of the 'Sunset Limited', while emergency crews comb the waters for bodies and collect evidence for the investigators.

INDEX